BIRDS OF THE
AFRICAN BUSH

BIRDS OF THE AFRICAN BUSH

Paintings by
RENA FENNESSY

Text by
LESLIE BROWN

COLLINS

St James's Place London

William Collins Sons & Co Ltd
London · Glasgow · Sydney · Auckland
Toronto · Johannesburg

First published 1975
© Illustrations Rena M Fennessy
© Text Leslie H Brown

ISBN 0 00 216069 2

Filmset in Garamond 156 and 201 by Tradespools Frome Somerset
Printed and bound in Spain by
E. Belgas, S. L. Ntra. Sra. de la Cabeza, 2 - Bilbao. Spain

To Leonard and Pat Gilmore
and to Barbara

Acknowledgments

The Artist wishes to express her thanks to Sir William Collins, who conceived the idea of this book, to the Trustees and Director of the Kenya National Museum who made it possible by kindly loaning specimens, and to Alec Forbes-Watson, ornithologist, for his help and advice in producing the pictures.

Both artist and author are deeply indebted to Barbara Brown for her constant support and for typing the manuscript, and to Peter Squelch for all his invaluable assistance and encouragement.

Contents

Contents

Introduction

When one looks at the grey, spiky, apparently lifeless thornbush of Africa in the sizzling noonday in the dry season one wonders how it can support life at all. The low trees stand there leafless, their dead-looking branches giving little real shade. Beneath, small shrubs seem wilted and battered, their leaves drying and falling. In the spaces between, whitish dead grass stands in sere contrast to baked black clay or patches of red sandy soil. Nothing much seems to move, and the shrilling of cicadas is often the only evidence of life. A puff of wind rustles the dead leaves and rattles a pod or two; and maybe the red column of a dust devil marches over the landscape lifting in its vortex bits of lost-looking debris, which flutter feebly back to earth some miles away.

Push a little way into the bush, and try to break one of those dead-looking stems to ease your passage and you find it is not only alive, but armed, and apparently vicious. Acacias hook your clothing and skin; one very common one is justly called "wait a bit" thorn, because you can only escape its clutch by a careful withdrawal, bit by bit. Commiphoras, grey-green, scaly looking, semi-succulent trees, bear stiff long spikes on their branches; and Euphorbias have both acid latex and thorns. In thickets beware the stiff-leaved bayonet aloe, *Sansevieria*, for if you try to walk among it your skin may be pierced as if by a dagger, leaving a deep puncture. Only the annual grasses are actually dead; and they often have awned seeds that attach themselves with fiendish ingenuity to any clothing, and can bore through it into your skin if not watched. It takes skill and experience to walk twenty yards through thick thornbush without losing a little blood. It is a hostile place.

Yet despite what it seems, it is far from lifeless or dead. It supports abundant wildlife, including the largest known populations of the world's largest land mammal, the elephant. It is the favourite home of the uncertain rhinoceros and of the Apollo of the antelopes, the lesser kudu. Giraffes browse in it, as do the long-necked gerenuk and the diminutive dikdik, whose pencil-thin legs and tiny hooves can cut like knives. All these animals, and birds too, rest in the shade at mid-day; and if you get out a comfortable chair and do likewise you will begin to see some of the bush birds going quietly about their business.

Birds are extraordinarily abundant in the bush. There can be as many as 40 per acre, a density as high as that in a temperate forest. Moreover, since few trees are more than twenty-five feet high, and most are much less, the majority of birds are fairly easily visible, not hidden among leaves in the top of giant trees, nor even, usually, concealed and skulking among impenetrable leafy thickets. Some species do skulk among shrubs near the ground; but even they come out in the open much more than, for instance, do larks in the long plains grass or greenbuls in forest undergrowth. Many species feed in the open patches of nearly bare ground, while others regularly hunt from treetops. The occasional tall tree, such as a baobab or a big Acacia, acts as a magnet for almost any bird that passes that way. In the mid-day heat you may as well recline in the shade yourself, for that way more birds will come to you than you would see by struggling through the bush looking for them.

If you lie there quiet, sooner or later a hornbill will fly into your tree, or a roller will perch on its upper branches. A shrike, or a small warbler may alight on the leafage and purposefully and silently make its way through, up, and round the tree, seeking tiny insects you yourself cannot see. In any baobab tree there are likely to be the thorny stick nests of buffalo weavers; and many large acacias are festooned with the dry grass nests of sparrow-weavers. Holes in such trees will almost certainly be the homes of glossy starlings or rollers; and in the upper branches there may well be a big pile of sticks, the nest of some bird of prey. The longer you sit quiet, the more you will see; a chair, a table with cool drinks, and slow quiet movements will not appreciably disturb the birds that come to the tree, though they may be aware of and curious about your presence.

Towards evening, as the day cools, activity in the bush increases. Large animals move out of the shade and begin to feed, perhaps moving towards water, though some such as gerenuk and lesser kudu do not need it. Birds move about much more freely, feeding

Birds of the African Bush

eagerly in the cool of the evening before roosting for the night. Towards dusk francolins call, and a Morning Warbler may sing a phrase or two. As dusk falls, the birds of the night take over. The African scops owl starts to give his little ventriloquial trill, a sound dear to all bush lovers. The Pearl-spotted Owlet utters his strange, eldritch mew; a nightjar or two flits about and calls from a bare space or a path; and high-pitched piping calls betray the whereabouts of the largely nocturnal coursers. A camp-fire is then both a comfort and a safeguard against inquisitive or blundering large animals; you can sleep like a baby, alone under your tree, without fear.

"Bush" is a loosely used word, applied in various parts of the world to anything from quite a tall forest to semi-desert. Here we are talking about the great tracts of semi-arid grass woodland and thornbush that cover perhaps four million square miles in Africa, from the Atlantic coast in a broad band south of the Sahara to Ethiopia and then south and east through Somalia and Kenya to Tanzania. Such thornbush and low savanna reappears in South Africa, again covering great tracts. One could be transported from Senegal to Somalia and to the Transvaal without noticing much difference in the general make-up of the bush, the low spiky trees, whitish dead grass, succulents and tall termite hills. Visibility is seldom more than about fifty yards, so that in flat country one can be hopelessly lost in half a mile from a known point. Trees look all the same; termite hills all seem instantly recognisable as the one seen a few minutes ago from another angle. Even old hands can get lost; and it's a bad place to be lost in, for surface water is scarce and widely scattered in the dry season, and it is hot from nine in the morning till four in the afternoon. This country must be treated with respect, and some caution; but if you learn your way about in it you soon come to love it.

There is a sense of peace and remoteness here; it is the epitome of a wilderness. The rainfall is too scanty to support dense human populations, and people you meet may often be pleasant honey-hunting types who, if you can speak their language, will probably be able to impart a wide store of knowledge, and will certainly prevent you from getting lost. Some of the bush people can put a name to any tree, grass, bird or animal; others are less knowledge-able. They leave their traces even in what seems to be uninhabited wilderness; honey hives hung in trees, an occasional pile of ashes at a good camp site; "bau" petroglyphs on rocks showing that by-gone people played that ancient game centuries ago; even hollows in rocky hills where hunters have used a pestle to grind arrow poison. Abandoned grind stones, that make admirable bird baths if you can lift them into your car, testify that such areas often were once inhabited, the people gone, died out many years past, and that the all-enveloping bush can return. Most trees are not very large or old; but the big baobabs are reckoned among the oldest living things. They look changeless, ancient. A 500-year-old baobab is a mere tooth-pick compared to the smooth grey barrel of an old colossus, that yields its life to nothing but the tusks of hungry elephants.

Since such vast tracts of Africa are covered by this kind of country, it is no surprise to find that many of the bush birds have a wide distribution. Of the 24 pictured in this book only a few are relatively local in North east Africa, and even most of these are found over a vast tract of country. Such birds as the Namaqua Dove, Little Bee Eater, Superb Starling and White-crowned Shrike can be found from Cape Province to the Sudan and west to Senegal. A few others such as the Golden-breasted Starling are more local, found in East Africa, Ethiopia and Somalia. There is no good reason why any of these birds should be confined to a small area, since the habitat is similar, and they can move freely within it. Thus they are generally common and widespread. No bird in our list is hard to find, and many are constant and obvious companions of the bush lover almost wherever he may be.

Their often startling beauty is more surprising. Somehow one feels that the birds of this dry, leafless looking country should be drab, brown or grey – and quiet. But they are not. Their portraits speak for themselves. Among the 24 species illustrated are two hot candidates – the Lilac-breasted Roller and the Golden-breasted Starling – for the title of Africa's most beautiful bird. Several others, notably the gaudy, perky, slightly meretricious Superb Starling, and the exquisite male of the Beautiful Sunbird make envious bird watchers form northern climates gasp in pleased astonishment. None is unattractive or dull, though

Introduction

one or two need a close look to appreciate them. The subtle shading and fine marking of a nightjar, or a scops owl perched against a tree bole, looking like rock or lichen, need a close look. The Namaqua Dove is surely one of the neatest and most graceful of all its family. Even the hornbills, the big Buffalo Weavers, and the White-crowned Shrikes that are among the most obvious of bush birds are not to be despised.

Birdsong is not a marked feature of the bush. There are a few good singers such as the Morning Warbler, which delights the listener at dawn from every thicket. There are a few pleasant calls to be heard, such as the metallic ringing "deet-deet-deet-deet" of the Nubian Woodpecker or the rattling morning laugh of the Grey-headed Kingfisher. But the beautiful starlings and spectacular rollers have harsh or wheezy voices, as do the Buffalo Weavers. Many birds are almost silent; the Blue-naped Mousebirds betray their presence only by a sad little "wheeee" as they take flight. The hornbills sob from treetops, even in the heat of the day; and the most unlikely noises of all are made by the Red-and-Yellow Barbets, whose astonishing cackling duets reveal their whereabouts as they rise in the morning and prepare for bed.

One must see the seasons though to get the best out of the bush. In the dry season the air is often full of haze, the product of innumerable fires and dustdevils. It seems lifeless and dead, and so remains for many long months. Then, at the end of the dry season, some of the trees awaken to unexpected life. Acacias blossom before they grow their new leaves, so that for large stretches the bush looks like a gigantic apple orchard. The trees then hum with bees, and birds seek the small insects drawn to the sweet-scented flowers. Parasitic, mistletoe-like plants, *Loranthus*, hang on many branches and produce quantities of tubular blooms beloved by sunbirds; later their sticky fruits are spread from tree to tree by small barbets and other fruit-eaters.

As the heat of the late dry season increases so the thunderheads build up in the sky, threatening rain every afternoon. For a time it does not fall, or a thin curtain of falling water that evaporates before it hits the ground appears beneath the blackness of the cloud. At night the flicker of lightning shows that it is raining somewhere far away. Then, one evening, or sometimes in the small hours when you do not expect it, the threatening rumble of thunder and an approaching black pall shows that the real thing is at last on its way. Batten down the tent, make sure the ditch is deep enough, tighten the guys and await the dramatic splendour of the storm. Before it, a half gale flings dust and debris in a red, billowing cloud. The first heavy drops follow a lull in the wind; and in a minute the battering rain falls on the dry earth, first laying the dust, then gathering in runnels and depressions, and finally rushing off down stream in turbid, debris-laden floods that last only an hour or two after the rain stops, if that. The thunder and lightning can be terrifying, yet awesomely beautiful, especially at night. The storm soon passes, and you will awaken to a world undergoing almost instant change.

The hungry red soil sucks up the moisture and steams as the day warms up. The air is clear, washed clean of all dust so that from a hilltop you may see a hundred miles to distant blue mountains. At midday clouds are building up again to herald another storm; and if you are in an out of the way place, with river beds and sticky black soil between you and a more solid road it may be time to make a bolt for it before that next storm falls. If you have picked your camp aright, however, you are about to witness a re-awakening far more swift and dramatic than the slow, reluctant budding and greening of the northern spring.

In the dawn after the rain the birds sing and call as they have not done for months. The rainy season will be short and sharp, so there is no time to waste. Most of the birds in the bush breed in the rains, or towards the end when seeds are abundant. They get on with nest-building as if at a signal. Guineafowl, hitherto in flocks, run about in separate pairs. Weavers go to and fro collecting grass, though those that make true woven nests often must wait until broad, green grass blades are available. They do not have to wait long. The first good storm starts a flush of vegetative growth that literally greens the bush in twenty-four hours and in a week transforms the dead looking trees into luxuriant green leaf and flowers. Insects are not far behind; and on the night after the first storm you will undoubtedly be plagued by masses of big, blundering scarab beetles and little brown beady beetles about

Birds of the African Bush

half an inch long. They may get in your soup; but if you are lucky an eagle owl may come to the circle of your light, and gorge himself (or herself) on the feast so conveniently gathered for him.

Ten days later the bush is in full leaf. More rain has brought on the grass in spaces between, and shrubs are flowering. Every bird is busy with nesting, the courting male hornbills flap their wings in absurd postures, and the thickets are rich with the song of Morning Warblers at dawn and dusk. Cuckoos, unseen and unheard in the dry season, suddenly become obvious: the Didric Cuckoo, the Pied Crested or Jacobin with its maniacal laugh, and the Black, whose melancholy "whooo-wheee-whay" can be translated as a despairing "I'm-so-sick!" The place that seemed so lifeless a few weeks before is bustling with an extravagant outburst of life; it was there all the time, waiting only for the rain to come.

A month or so later things have calmed down. Birds are now feeding young rather than building, streams are flowing in dry river beds and the bush is lush and green in a way one could not dream of in the dry season. At the end of the short rainy season the sky is clear, the air scented; now is the time to climb a mountain and see the cloud shadows marching over the plains, once the morning mist on the hilltop has dispersed. Pick your time and place, and you will be unlikely to be washed out; and you can enjoy days of glorious sunshine with birds and animals all around.

A month later, and it is all over. The leaves of the commiphoras yellow to autumn colours with the coming drought, the fine leaflets of the acacias fall like a gentle nutritious rain to feed the still lush grasses growing in their shade. Even the baobab, after a brief flush of leaves and unlikely-looking waxy flowers, that last for a night and are pollinated by bats and bush babies, reverts to its old grey naked self. Birds are more abundant than ever, for the broods of the weavers and guineafowl form into flocks with their parents, pairs of francolins have become coveys, and many small birds are obviously feeding young out of the nest. But there is now no need to sing, for breeding is done and the drying bush is now silent. It awaits the time when it must retreat before the oncoming dry season, when the leaves have dropped, the stems of the grass dry to a lifeless white, and the bush stands there once more naked, grey, hostile, and resembling a company of skeletons. The change is gradual but certain; and the birds and beasts of the bush become silent and withdrawn, once more hard to see.

Yet now is the time when the bush lover returns to his favourite places, inaccessible perhaps during the rains, to camp again round a fire beneath a well-loved tree, and chew the fat endlessly into the night. Even now there is life going on. Birds of prey mainly breed in the dry season, as do nightjars; although they are insectivorous, the rains make breeding uncomfortable on the ground. The fascination of the bush does not pall at any time of year, and a lover of nature finds peace and solace here, dry or wet. The birds are always there; there are just some times of the year when it is easier to see them, and appreciate how many and how beautiful they are.

BIRDS OF THE AFRICAN BUSH

1 The Superb Starling
Spreo superbus

If the Superb Starling lived in Europe, and was rare, people would flock to any locality in which it was found in order to see it. As it is, in East Africa this abundant, tame, bold and gregarious creature of brilliant plumage is virtually taken for granted and ignored. It is yet another classic example, if one were needed, of the way in which beautiful, interesting and common species that could be studied without difficulty are neglected in favour of something rarer and perhaps less beautiful.

In fact, more is known about this species now than has yet been published, for at least one enthusiast is now studying their social habits in detail. However, it will be some time before these are available. From preliminary results it appears that Superb Starlings live in extended families, with the grown young staying on with the parents and perhaps helping to feed the next brood. This is typical of the surprise that sometimes occurs when a common and apparently well-known bird is thoroughly studied for the first time.

The Superb Starling is well-named, for it is exquisitely beautiful. It may lack the beauty of form and grace of movement to put it in the top class; but the brilliant blues and green-blues of the upper side contrast smartly with the chestnut belly. It lives in the same areas as two very close relatives, Shelley's Starling and Hildebrandt's Starling; and some have difficulty in distinguishing these. However, in adult plumage the Superb's white cummerbund immediately distinguishes it. The young lack the white cummerbund, and are duller generally; but their dark eyes at once distinguish them from the white-eyed adult Shelley's Starling, or the red-eyed Hildebrandt's. All three do not usually occur together, and the Superb Starling is more adaptable in its choice of habitat than either. Shelley's is normally a bird of thornbush proper, while Hildebrandt's likes grassy plains with some trees rather than dense thornbush. The Superb Starling occurs anywhere from dry combretum savannas to real thornbush.

Abundant, widespread, perky and cheeky, but wary, they know just how far they can go. They are one of the birds most easily tamed at lodges and hotels, where they will hop on the table for crumbs. Even round a camp they are soon down on the ground looking for scraps,

The Superb Starling

and no keen photographer need lack his picture for long. They are probably among the most photographed of all land birds in East Africa.

Although they come readily for all sorts of scraps and crumbs, and apparently can digest all these foreign substances without harm, their natural food is insects, mainly taken on the ground, and including a large number of termites. Termites, in fact, take a real beating from many of the bush birds. Superb Starlings also eat other insects, and some fruit, though they rarely congregate in a fruiting tree like some other starlings, and are not really dependent on fruit. Amongst other insects they eat ants, notably the harvester ants which collect grass seed; so it is perhaps not so surprising that they should be one of only three species of birds in Africa so far observed at the curious behaviour known as "anting".

When anting, these starlings pick up a large ant, in the single case so far observed of the sub-family *Camponotinae*, some of which are stingless but store large quantities of formic acid in their bodies, which they can spray out when alarmed. The starlings pick up these ants and, spreading their wings, stroke the underside and upperside of the wing, and also the back. Alternatively, they crouch in a trance-like posture, with wings spread, and with the head on its side, gazing at the sky. They hold an ant in the bill for a minute or so; but when done with this strange almost hypnotic performance can apparently pull themselves together smartly, snap their wings shut, make a short hop, and resume their normal alert upright stance. The reason for anting is not yet fully understood in any species; but seems most likely to be part of feather care, in which the bird applies, through the presumably unwilling ant, a squirt of insect repellent to its plumage.

Superb Starlings breed in the rains in most of their habitat. They may use a hole in a tree, an old buffalo weavers nest, or may be forced to make their own nests. These are clumsy domed bundles of grass, enclosed with thorny sticks with a hole at the side, and they are usually situated in a very thorny bush which may sometimes have been pruned into tight-packed topiary work by giraffes or other browsing animals. Van Someren believed that they made large nest of thorny sticks on branches, like buffalo weavers, and then built up a ramp of thorny sticks along the branch which would help to deter mammalian predators. However, it seems possible that in such situations the starlings have used a buffalo weaver's nest and lined it with grass, though they may add more sticks to the defences of thorny sticks already placed there by the buffalo weavers. Buffalo weavers actually seem to link some starlings with true weaver birds. Anyway, we know far too little about the nesting habits of both.

Four, occasionally five, glossy blue eggs are laid, and are incubated, probably by both sexes, for fourteen days. The fledging period is not recorded in any available book. Most eggs are laid in or just after the rains, so that the family parties with young are about when insect food is abundant. The young remain with their parents for some time, perhaps even after they become fully adult themselves; they acquire full adult plumage about six months after leaving the nest, their eye-colour changing to white at the same time.

Length seven inches, sexes alike

2 The Grey-headed Kingfisher
Halcyon leucocephala

The bush-lover waking in the cool freshness of the pre-dawn glimmer knowns that certain birds will be the first to greet the rising sun. The Grey-headed Kingfisher and its relative the Striped Kingfisher are two of these. Well before the sun is up, a joyous ringing rattling shout, hard to describe, but to my mind like "yeemp – trrrrrrr", descending in pitch, resounds from the top of some tree. The glasses reveal the grey head, deep chestnut belly of the Grey-headed Kingfisher perched on his morning branch – for we assume it is the male that sings.

Kingfishers are usually thought to eat fish – probably because the only species which occurs in Europe *does* live on fish. In fact, however, the majority of the African kingfishers are insectivorous, notably those that live in the savanna or forest. They may eat some fish or frogs; but their staple is insects such as grasshoppers, which they usually catch on the ground. In the bush at least three species – the Grey-headed, the Striped, and Brown-hooded all live mainly on insects. Several other *Halcyon* kingfishers living in forests or mangroves do the same; and of the nineteen species of African kingfishers only six really depend on fish.

The Grey-headed Kingfisher does some of both. Its favourite haunts in East Africa are along riversides where it can sometimes catch fish in shallow streams; but it also lives happily in the dry bush miles from any water. In Nigerian savannas I have found them nesting in the mouth of an antbear burrow two miles from any water. The distance they move from permanent water perhaps depends on the total rainfall. In broad leaved savannas and woodlands they are likely to be found further from any possible water than in the thornbush, where they are normally found among the larger timber along watercourses, permanent or temporary.

Care is needed to distinguish the Grey-headed from two close relatives, the Brown-hooded and Woodland Kingfishers. The Brown-hooded generally inhabits drier country, lacks the chestnut belly, and is paler, more turquoise blue on the wings. The Woodland Kingfisher is paler blue, has a white belly, and a good view shows that its lower mandible is black, whereas the whole massive bill of the Grey-headed Kingfisher is bright red. In flight

The Grey-headed Kingfisher

the Grey-headed is a much brighter, deeper cobalt blue than either. The flash of those brilliant wings as a Grey-headed Kingfisher flits down to the waterside is one of the unforgettable delights of any streamside camp in the middle of the day, when little else stirs. The kingfishers rest unobtrusive in the shade of a big tree; but catch food whenever they have a good chance and are hungry.

Grey-headed Kingfishers occur over a vast tract of savanna and thorn-bush in Africa. In some areas they are permanently resident, in others they migrate. In central Nigerian savannas they move in southwards in the early dry season, breed and depart with the coming of the rains; some apparently breed in the rains further north. In such areas they therefore breed when small fish in clear shrunken streams are easier to see and catch; but when breeding in an antbear burrow miles from water the same species must subsist on insects not so easy to find, in bush which has probably been burned black. In southern Africa the Grey-headed Kingfisher is also migratory, occurring between September and March, breeding and departing northwards, showing almost the opposite seasonal pattern to Nigeria, for this is the *wet* season in southern woodlands. Near the Equator it seems to be resident year-round; and breeds both in wet and dry seasons.

Some of the *Halcyon* kingfishers have so far departed from true kingfisher tradition that they breed in holes in trees; such include the Woodland and the Striped Kingfisher. The Grey-headed, however, makes a perfectly normal burrow in a bank, digging a fresh one each year; it varies from true fish-eating riverside kingfishers chiefly in using also banks in dry country lacking water. The burrows are three to four feet deep, slightly curving from entrance to nesting chamber, too narrow and long for a human arm to feel the eggs. Personally I am always a little reluctant to thrust a bare arm into a dark hole in a bank, for there may well be a cobra at the end of it. However, if the kingfisher emerges – as it usually does if the burrow is occupied – then one need not fear such other inhabitants. Normally 3–4 eggs are laid; they are round and white like those of all kingfishers, and when fresh they show a pale delicate pink through the shell.

Again, although this is a very widespread and well-known bird, it does not seem to have been studied in any detail at the nest. No doubt this is partly due to the difficulty of seeing what goes on at the back of a deep hole. No one to my knowledge has so far dug a covered trench at the back of the hole, and carefully opened the nest chamber from the rear so as to see what goes on, as has been done with some other hole-nesting kingfishers and with bee-eaters. The incubating bird usually signals occupation of the burrow by its departure, though quite how the bird detects the approach of an intruder from within the dark hole is obscure. Possibly both sexes incubate; and certainly both feed the young at short intervals, feeding being at least as common in midday heat as early in the morning or evening. When small, the young are fed in the chamber at the back of the burrow; but when large they come to the entrance to be fed. They cast up the hard undigested remains of insects; but the nests are usually quite clean and dry, not as foul as those of true fish-eating kingfishers.

Those who camp by a riverside where they can watch a pair of nesting Grey-headed Kingfishers may therefore reflect that almost any detail they record is likely to be unpublished. So often, common species are little known; and in kingfishers, as in rollers, this is all the more curious because they are conspicuous, familiar, and beautiful.

Length eight inches, sexes alike

3 The Little Bee-eater
Merops pusillus

Bee-eaters are apparently a very successful avian design, basically all much the same shape, differing mainly in size and colour, and all aerial hunters of bees and other insects. Most are colonial, breeding in large, sometimes spectacular colonies in riverbanks, or in flat ground. A few forest species are more solitary; and so is the Little Bee-eater of the bush.

Little Bee-eaters are everywhere through the dry African savannas. Not confined to the neighbourhood of water, they breed in any available stream or roadside bank, rise of ground, anthill, or antbear burrow, even the old hole of a rodent. In Sudan, long ago, Heuglin stated that they used old weaver-bird nests. It seems wildly unlikely; but could happen in flat wet country, where banks are scarce. Heuglin has been doubted before, and found right after all.

At most one finds a few pairs close to one another, never a packed colony as with many bee-eaters. One result of this is that although Little Bee-eaters are probably the most abundant and widespread of all African species, they are comparatively little known. They have never yet been studied from a covered pit dug behind the burrows to watch what goes on in the nest chamber.

However, their general ways are familiar to anyone who has spent much time in the bush; one sees them almost anywhere. They normally perch on a low branch, a grass stem, or a dead weed, and from there make short sorties to catch insects. They are remarkably successful, spotting the insect, flying ten to twenty yards, to catch it with an audible snap of the bill, and usually returning to the same or a nearby perch. A cautious approach in a car, and a big lens will usually provide a good colour picture in under a quarter of an hour, for they are tame, and not easily disturbed in a chosen hunting ground. When they alight again on the perch they often wag the tail up and down, and utter little squeaking calls, as if satisfied with their efforts.

Like most bee-eaters Little Bee-eaters eat bees, though are less exclusively dependent on bees than some. About 70% of all insects taken are ants, bees and wasps; and about one in

The Little Bee-eater

five is a true bee of the genus *Apis*. Not all of these insects can sting or bite; but the bee-eater knows how to deal with any that can. On returning to its perch with a bee it grips it firmly by the narrow waist between abdomen and thorax, and first bangs the head hard against the branch. Then, having stunned the bee, it swiftly shifts the grip to the tip of the abdomen, and rubs this against the branch, so disposing of the sting. All insects have their heads banged; but only venomous ones have their abdomen rubbed against the branch to remove the sting. Evidently the bee-eaters knows at once what is dangerous and what not. However, the harmless male drone bee, which has no sting, is treated in much the same way as the stinging female worker; the bee-eater plays safe. Apparently even a young bee-eater, hand-reared, never having seen a bee in its life, knows how to deal with it without getting stung.

These details have not all been observed in Little Bee-eaters but they seem to behave much as do other bee-eaters, studied in greater detail. So it's worth watching a Little Bee-eater with some care when the chance comes. It is a joy to do so, for the graceful little creature, brilliant green above, with a bright yellow throat separated from chestnut or saffron under-parts by a black choker, is entirely charming, not least because it is so confiding and easy to watch.

Little Bee-eaters are normally resident in tropical Africa, but in some areas migrate. In Malawi the residents are increased by breeding visitors in August; but where these go when they have finished breeding is not known – presumably further north. One never sees Little Bee-eaters in such obvious migrating flocks as, for instance, the European Bee-eater, or the White-throated Bee-eater, which migrates within the tropics.

Few people have the heart to dig out bee-eater nesting holes just to see what's in them; and those of the Little Bee-eater are so narrow that one can hardly see what's inside even with a torch. However, it seems that they breed both in rainy and in dry seasons, more often the latter. Bees are more obvious and abundant during the rains when many flowering trees and bushes yield honey; but many acacias come into heavy scented flower just before the rains, so that Little Bee-eaters would not lack food then either.

The nest holes are 18 inches to four feet deep, and as in all bee-eaters the eggs, two to six, are white, roundish, and glossy. For so small a bird the 29-day incubation period is astonishingly long; and the young stay in the nest, among the undigested remains of insects, for another 29 days. They then emerge, and the whole family perches together, the young being fed by both parents. Sometimes, honey-guides manage to lay an egg in a bee-eater hole, in which case the young bee-eaters are doomed.

In some colonial bee-eaters the males outnumber the females; and in the Red-throated Bee-eater "helpers" assist the mated pair at the nest. Little Bee-eaters have equal sex-ratio, and no helpers have been seen. However, much remains to be learned about the nesting of this commonest of all bee-eaters. As usual, that which is common, easy to observe, is taken for granted.

Length six inches, sexes alike

4 The Purple Grenadier

Uraeginthus ianthinogaster

One of the great minor pleasures of bush life is the abundance of pretty little small birds, notably Estrildine weavers or weaver-finches. Often, these are not only as common, but also far easier to see in and round human habitations as in uninhabited thickets, for they tend to come to spilled grain and other such scraps round villages. Here one may see a selection of manikins, waxbills, pytilias, fire finches and cordon-bleus, and with them, very often, the Grenadier. This is one of the largest of this group of little weaver-finches, and one of the most decorative, though they are all pretty in their way when one has a good look at them.

Grenadiers are presumably so called because of the rich purple hue of the male's underside and tail; perhaps some imaginative Frenchman had a hand in it. Generally, one first sees them disappearing into a thicket, with a flash of that purple rear end. However, they are not shy, and soon emerge again to feed; or they may be seen cautiously peering from inside the thicket. They are one of the weaver-finches that also occur in uninhabited bush far from human habitations, and they can survive here in waterless places perhaps because, like so many other bush birds, they feed on harvester termites. Round houses they will soon learn to come to a bird table; and if one uses a favourite camping site it is worth while to scatter a few handfuls of small grain or meal to attract these and others.

They are less gregarious than some of the other weaver finches such as waxbills or manikins, which go about in small excitable flocks. Grenadiers are usually found in pairs, or at most in small parties, which may be family groups of parents and their young. They are sociable with some other small weaver finches, and feed on the ground alongside cordon-bleus and fire finches. However, they are more retiring than many; and it is not so easy to get a really good clear view of the beautiful male.

In South Africa most of these little birds are firmly called waxbills, irrespective of whether they have bills like red sealing wax or not. Grenadiers of both sexes have red bills; but only the male has the purple cheek patches which give it the name Blue-eared Waxbill in

The Purple Grenadier

southern Africa. They used to be in a genus of their own, *Granatina*, but have now been lumped with Cordon-bleus (or should one say Cordons-bleu) in *Uraeginthus*; perhaps this is a good idea, for there does not seem to be very much difference in their habits.

The whole group of waxbills, grenadiers and others belong to one of the two main sub-divisions of weaver birds, known as Estrildine weavers after the genus *Estrilda* which includes the typical waxbills. They are mainly African but a few species also occur in India and the East. They are not weavers at all, in that they do not weave a nest like any of the typical Ploceid weavers or Malimbes. They all make ball-shaped nests of loose grass heads, in which they both roost and breed and they lay pure white eggs. One of their more engaging peculiarities is that the young all have characteristic markings inside their mouths which enables their parents to recognise – nearly infallibly – which mouth to stuff with food and which not. There are nearly as many of these Estrildine weavers as of Ploceids; but they are all small or very small, and none make a proper woven nest.

I cannot find much detail written on the breeding habits of the Grenadier; but the nests are usually within thick bush and therefore not easy to find. They are generally quite close to the ground, and are large loose balls, made of grass heads outside and lined with feathers. A favourite grass to use is Guinea grass, but the fluffy heads of *Rhynchelytrum repens*, a common pioneer weed grass of rosy hue when in young flower are also much used. The nests are built by both sexes, and when the female has laid her three to five eggs and has begun to sit the male continues to bring feathers to add to the lining. He also shares the incubation of the eggs; this appears normal in most waxbills, whether or not, as in the Grenadier, the male is much more brightly coloured than the female.

The young hatch in about two weeks, and have those characteristic markings inside their mouths by which the feeding parent is supposed to be able to recognise them. However, among these weaver-finches a cunning form of nest-parasitism has developed, in which the long-tailed whydahs lay eggs in the nests of others, leaving them to be hatched by the Grenadiers or whatever other species is concerned. The parasitism is, however, less malevolent than that of cuckoos or honey guides, in that the young whydah, when hatched, does not throw out or kill its nest mates, but remain with them till it flies. Thus, unless there is an acute shortage of food, the young Grenadiers may not suffer from the presence of the young whydah. The Purple Grenadier in East Africa is the only known host of Fischer's Straw-tailed Whydah, a rather scarce species; and in South Africa is parasitised by the Shaft-tailed Whydah, evidently a close relative of Fischer's. The young whydahs in either case are not detected by the parent Grenadiers because the markings on the inside of their mouths are very like, but not exactly identical to those of their hosts.

After the young leave the nest they quickly develop the plumage of the adults; and are probably able to breed in the season following their first flight. In East Africa the Grenadiers normally nest in the rains, perhaps because insect food for the young is then available, while a plentiful supply of grass and weed seeds inevitably follows, and aids survival through the dry season.

Length five and a half inches, male and female (above)

5 The Blue-naped Mousebird
Colius macrourus

Mousebirds or Colies are an exclusively African family. The six species occur in every African habitat except dense forest and stark desert. All mousebirds are about the same size, go about in parties, have long stiff tails and crests, and are generally drab or dull coloured. They may be called mousebirds because of their habit of creeping about like mice inside thick cover. They perch in unusual attitudes because their legs join the body high up and well forward; and because all four toes point forward, though the outer two can be reversed at will to grip a twig. Often, they hang on a perch, with the feet and shoulders at about the same level; and they are extraordinarily nimble, able to move swiftly from one perch to another and attain a great variety of attitudes.

The Blue-naped Mousebird is one of the most widespread of all, inhabiting a great tract of semi-arid country from Senegal to East-central Africa. It is also perhaps the most attractive of the whole group, much neater in plumage than the very abundant Speckled Mousebird, grey with a bright blue nape and red beak. Yet it is very little known throughout its vast range. This is partly because it lives in countries where bird watchers are scarce; but also because it is a shy bird, difficult to observe for long.

One becomes aware that Blue-naped Mousebirds are about without seeing them, for they advertise their whereabouts by a long drawn, mournful whistle, "Sueeeeee". On following up the call, usually all that one sees is a tight little bunch of long-tailed grey birds fleeing like arrows through the tops of the bush. One must be very quiet and careful to obtain a really good view of them as they feed working through the branches of a tree. In thick cover they are hard to see; and usually when you have seen them they have seen you, and are ready to leave. Why they should be so shy is obscure, for their behaviour is unlike that of the ubiquitous and extremely bold Speckled Mousebird.

In Kenya and Uganda these mousebirds are more easily observed round Lake Victoria than in the eastern thornbush. Parties used regularly to pass through my garden at Kisumu; but they were noticeably shyer than the Speckled Mousebirds found in the same area.

The Blue-naped Mousebird

I never found a nest; and even when nesting in game wardens' gardens these secretive birds have apparently escaped any detailed observation.

Nests are usually made inside a thorny bush; but I have seen one on an open acacia branch, and others are recorded in similar situations. They are small cup like structures, with a base of twigs, lined with finer material, shredded grass, rootlets, even green leaves or flower heads, much smaller and neater than the untidy nests of the Speckled Mousebird. The two or three eggs are white, scrawled and speckled with dark brown or dark red, sometimes unmarked. The sitting bird often has the tail cocked almost vertically; such a long appendage must be inconvenient in a small cup nest. He or she sits very tight, but if one pushes into the bush, creeps out and leaves from the far side.

Although little detail is known about Blue-naped Mousebirds the habits of all mousebirds are so similar that we can expect them to conform. They regularly move about in parties of ten to thirty; and if a party is broken up they will later reform. They love basking in the sun, perched on high twigs where they can easily slip into thick cover at any sign of danger. They also love dustbathing, and can be seen in the evening in groups shuffling in loose dust on roads. They go to roost together, and sleep in tight-packed clusters inside a bush. Large flocks may break up into two or three smaller bunches to roost. Roosting in such tight bunches may, in some mousebirds, help to maintain high temperatures; but this is hardly needed in the Blue-naped Mousebird, which lives in hot dry country.

Mousebirds feed mainly on fruit, and when fruit is short will strip green leaves, flowers, buds, or collect nectar. They are, for this reason, the despair of fruit growers; but are so clever and secretive that they usually manage to escape persecution. Shooting them quite quickly educates members of a flock; they return, but become very much more shy after seeing one or two of their number killed. Blue-naped Mousebirds usually are not a serious pest because they often live in country where little fruit can be grown.

Mousebirds go to bed early and get up late, though the Blue-naped is more likely to be seen early in the morning, like other birds of the bush. The members of a group preen each other; and captive mousebirds constantly beg for attention from their owners. They also learn to play with all sorts of objects. Constant calling among flocks keeps the members together, and is apparently much more important for cohesion than sight. This might be expected among birds which, in danger, tend to hide in thick bushes.

The gregarious habits of mousebirds may even continue when breeding. They separate into individual pairs; but several often nest quite close together. Both parents are very attentive to both eggs and young, and in some species have literally to be pushed off the nest if one wants to examine the contents. Known incubation periods are short, 11–13 days, and fledging periods, in which both parents feed the young, and brood them even when feathered, about 17 days. Thus, a pair of mousebirds can build a nest and rear a brood in little over a month. Whether these general rules also apply to Blue-naped Mousebirds remains to be seen. They give one an impression, by their shyness and swift movements, that they are rather different, at least to Speckled Mousebirds; but anyone who has the chance to watch them at a nest can find out.

Length fourteen inches, sexes alike. Courtesy, John G. Tremlett, Esq., Kenya

Réna

6 The Pygmy Falcon
Poliohierax semitorquatus

Not quite the smallest bird of prey, since four species of still smaller falconets occur in forests of Borneo and Malaysia, the Pygmy Falcon is still the smallest African raptor, weighing only about 60 grams. It is barely bigger than a large shrike, and looks rather like one at first. However, a closer look reveals the hooked beak and taut muscular body of the true predator and one realises that this is altogether a more formidable creature than any shrike.

Pygmy Falcons are usually found singly or in pairs; if there are three or more they are probably a family party. Normally they are seen perching on some commanding stub or dead branch, or near the top of a tree. Approached, they depart with a direct, swift, undulating woodpecker-like flight, the white spots in the spread tail betraying their identity when they alight. They go about their business in a more purposeful manner than even the larger and more predatory shrikes.

They are true birds of the arid thornbush, not seen where the grass is long among big broad leaved trees. Once seen, they often allow close approach, and can be watched at leisure, especially if they have prey. One may see one or two in a morning, for they are not normally very common anywhere. They are more numerous in the Kalahari desert than anywhere in East Africa.

Pigmy Falcons often feed on insects, caught on the ground with a short swift rush. However, they also take small snakes, many lizards, a few mammals and occasional birds. Probably lizards are more important than insects by weight, especially when breeding. They kill their prey on the ground with a short dive, not in the grand manner of big falcons.

Male and female differ in plumage. She is only slightly bigger than he, but has a chestnut or maroon back, whereas his is pale grey. She displays her back at mating time. The white underside could help to make the perched falcon less conspicuous against the sky and so help it to catch lizards and mammals unaware. However, it takes many insects that could not see it anyhow until too late.

The Pygmy Falcon

No true falcons make their own nests; and Pygmy Falcons use the old or abandoned nests of weaver birds. The northern race, inhabiting the bush of East and North-east Africa, uses the large thorny nests of buffalo weavers. Buffalo weavers are as big as the falcon and likely to be pugnacious, so it is unlikely that rightful owners have their occupied dwellings usurped. The nests are used both for roosting and breeding; and contact with the harsh thorny structure makes the falcon's plumage worn and threadbare.

In South Africa, where the Pygmy Falcon has been studied in detail, it breeds almost exclusively in the huge communal nests of the Social Weaver. These nests, as big as a small haystack, and containing many nest chambers, are visible for miles. About one in four may be occupied by Pygmy Falcons, which appropriate several of the chambers, using them year-round, some for breeding, some for roosting. In this case the weavers are individually too small to resist the falcon; they are agitated and alarmed by them, and sometimes abandon a whole nest mass. The falcons may occasionally eat young weavers when prospecting nest-holes, but more likely benefit their hosts indirectly, by helping to repel snakes, which are the main enemies of these weavers.

Most falcons' eggs are a beautiful, freckled rich brick red. The Pygmy Falcon lays nearly white eggs showing that for aeons it has bred in dark enclosed places, and has reverted to laying the white or whitish eggs typical of hole-nesting birds. The few East African records suggest that it breeds here towards the end of the rains, when insects, rats and fledglings are likely to abound. In South Africa it breeds in the Kalahari in summer, August to February, laying eggs in the dry season but producing young in the rains.

Two to four eggs are laid, about three weeks after mating, at intervals of two days, so that the young are unequal in size. Both parents incubate, the female most; she is fed by the male, who continues to kill all prey needed till the young are feathered (at 21 days), after which the female takes her share. The combined incubation and fledging periods (about 28 and 30 days) is much the same as for Peregrines, ten times the weight of the Pygmy Falcon. A pair rears about two young from an average of three eggs laid, and the young remain with them for about two months; but can themselves breed when a year old. Rarely, a pair rears a second brood in a season.

Since the northern population of Pygmy Falcons depends on buffalo weavers for nesting accommodation, anything that reduces these birds also affects the falcon. In the Tsavo Park, where the elephants have destroyed most of the big trees favoured by buffalo weavers for nesting, the Pygmy Falcon then also becomes rare or disappears. However, the thornbush is vast; and in most of its north African range the Pygmy Falcon can still find abundant buffalo weaver's nests. Though there is thus no likelihood that this beautiful little falcon will become generally rare in the foreseeable future, it is always one of the more uncommon of the bush birds, and a special pleasure to see.

Length seven and a half inches, male and female (with chestnut back). Courtesy, John G. Tremlett, Esq., Kenya

7 The Didric Cuckoo

Chrysococcyx caprius

Cuckoos are always fascinating birds, by reason of their curious and slightly malevolent habits towards the hosts that rear their young. In Europe, one thinks of a cuckoo as a dull grey bird that says "Cuck-oo"; but in Africa the variety of cuckoos is great, they invade almost every habitat where there is another bird to parasitise, and some of them are brilliantly beautiful. The Didric Cuckoo is one of a group of small, metallic green cuckoos, of which the brightest gem is the forest-loving Emerald Cuckoo. When seen in sunlight its coppery gloss still makes it a very beautiful bird. It gets its name from its rather quavering call "Dee-dee-diederick", which is uttered by displaying males. Females have a different call, a plaintive "deeea-deeea" or "weeeea". Anyway, there's no mistaking the male's call; and to me it begins with a D.

Didric Cuckoos (firmly called Diederick Cuckoos in South Africa) are not strictly confined to the bush country, but occur over a vast range of all sorts of habitats where they can find their hosts, nearly all weaver birds and bishop birds, occasionally wagtails. Since weavers are among the most ubiquitous birds in Africa the Didric Cuckoo is almost everywhere too. However, it avoids tall forest where there are few weavers. In bush country, because of the copious seed supply at the end of the rains, weavers abound so there are plenty of Didric Cuckoos too.

Not that anyone will see a Didric Cuckoo, except by luck, in the dry season. At that season all African cuckoos are silent and unobtrusive. They must often be there, for they cannot miraculously come out of the ground when rain falls; but one seldom sees them, and never hears them. They probably migrate from dry to moist areas when the need arises; certainly some cuckoos, notably the Pied Crested Cuckoo, perform remarkable migrations by unknown routes across the Indian Ocean to Africa. However, there is little positive information on the subject in tropical Africa.

Rain, as we said, releases the life of the bush. With the first heavy storms the grass begins to grow, and it is not long before weavers start building their nests. Almost at once the Didric Cuckoo makes its appearance. The males fly from tree to tree, plaintively calling, with tails

The Didric Cuckoo

spread, showing the conspicuous white spots on the outer feathers. They chase away other males by sheer pugnacity, and establish territories into which the females quietly come. They are duller than the males, lack the white eyebrow and are more barred beneath, but still beautiful. The males feed them with caterpillars, which seem to be the staple diet of many cuckoos in Africa. Having mated they set about finding a weaver's or sparrow's nest in which to lay their eggs.

Cuckoos are difficult birds to study; but have always had their devotees. The Didric Cuckoo has been extensively studied in South Africa by Rolf Jensen and Carl Vernon. Examining hundreds of weavers', bishops' and sparrows' nests they found that overall parasitism could vary from nil to two thirds of the nests, averaging about one nest in ten; evidently this could vary in other parts of Africa. Although individual nests of weavers are destroyed by the breeding of a cuckoo in them, the species concerned have adapted to this level of parasitism, and are not as a whole affected. Cuckoo and weaver host both thrive.

Among South African Didric Cuckoos too, there are at least three clans, technically called *gentes*, which lay different-coloured eggs and prefer to parasitise certain weaver species; The best marked of these is one which lays blue eggs and parasitises Red Bishop Birds; there may also be a fourth clan which lays white eggs and parasitises Cape Wagtails, not weavers. Bishop birds, which nest in grass, and Black-headed Weavers, which in tropical Africa nest in waterside reedbeds may be more heavily parasitised than some other species which nest high in trees such as the Village Weaver; but again, it is more difficult for humans to examine such high nests, and obtain those so important, significant figures.

Weavers object to the presence of Didric Cuckoos, and chase them away. Nevertheless, a female bent on laying an egg in a weaver's nest eventually manages to do so. She sometimes removes one of the eggs of the weaver, and may eat it. She enters the nest to lay, and does not put the egg into it after laying it elsewhere, as has sometimes been thought possible in cuckoos. Once the egg is in the nest, the weaver's brood is doomed. Up to three eggs, presumably not all laid by the same female cuckoo, have been found in one weaver's nest.

Young cuckoos all hatch in short periods, 12–13 days in the Didric Cuckoo. They are thus able to eject the unhatched eggs of their hosts, or the small chicks, by superior strength. The young Didric, hatching in deep weaver's nests, has more difficulty in throwing out the eggs of its hosts than some other cuckoos that lay in open nests, for instance of pipits; they are not strong enough to do it till they are 24 hours old. However, in the end, all the weavers eggs or small chicks are ejected and lie on the ground below. The young cuckoo then has the full attention of the female weaver, who would otherwise have to feed two or more of her own young.

Young Didric Cuckoos fly about 20 days after hatching, and are dependent on the weaver parent for another three weeks. In South Africa the adults arrive in the nesting areas about a month before laying, and depart soon after they have laid, at any rate before the young can fly. The fledged young thus have to find their own way to their winter quarters somewhere in tropical Africa. In our tropical East African thornbush we know less about it; but probably a similar pattern applies. After all, once the female has got rid of her eggs she has no reason to stay for she has no young to feed; they are looked after by the weavers. So, as the old English rhyme says "away she doth fly", to be followed, instinctively, by young who have never been there before.

Length seven and a half inches, male

8 The Lilac-breasted Roller
Coracias caudata

A candidate for the title of Africa's most beautiful bird should, to my mind, combine brilliant colour with grace of form; be a fair size so that an average person can appreciate the detail; and be fairly common. Many otherwise exquisite species are rather hard to see or rare; or are small, such as sunbirds, and consequently do not to me rate so high as larger birds. Ideally, the bird should also have a pleasant if not actually melodious voice. But that's a matter of opinion, for many of the most beautiful birds have harsh calls.

The Lilac-breasted Roller is the first of two hot contenders for this title found in the bush. That such a wealth of beauty should be available in this arid thorn country is itself eloquent – especially when one thinks that birds such as the Superb Starling are not even in my short list. It is both graceful and fairly large; perches often in the open on telegraph wires or stubs of dead trees; and is brilliantly beautiful, especially in flight. But there's no denying that it has a very harsh, grating voice, even if this is an integral part of its display flight, where it serves to attract attention.

Rollers as a group are all beautiful, fairly large, and mostly rather common. It is all the stranger that they do not seem to have been very intensively studied anywhere in Africa. The Lilac-breasted Roller occurs over a very large area of East and North-east Africa south to the Cape Province. In the south-central African woodlands it is replaced by the Racquet-tailed Roller, and from north Ethiopia westwards by the even more brilliant, but perhaps less subtly beautiful Abyssinian Roller. It certainly ought to be better known than any other roller, since it is the commonest and most widespread of any species living in parts of Africa also inhabited by ornithologists. Yet I know of no detailed study of this or, for that matter, any other resident African roller.

The brilliant beauty of the Lilac-breasted Roller was prized by the Matabele king Mzilikazi, who reserved its feathers for his own exclusive use. Like most rollers its back is brownish, but most of the plumage is light or dark blue, and the upper breast is a rich mauve. The outer tail feathers are long and black-tipped, contrasting with the rest of the blue tail. At

The Lilac-breasted Roller

rest it is much more brightly coloured, smaller, and more graceful than either the European or the Rufous-crowned Roller and at once differentiated by its forked long tail. Its true beauty is displayed only in flight, most strikingly in the frenzied, tumbling nuptial displays characteristic of the roller tribe generally. Then, the glorious contrast of dark and light blue in the wings flashes as the bird twirls round and round, or from side to side in scintillating aerobatics. One could scarcely miss such displays even if they were not advertised by harsh screams audible half a mile away.

Lilac-breasted Rollers are not found exclusively in thornbush; they are less characteristic of such country than the larger Rufous-crowned Rollers. They also live in light woodland with long grass, even in coastal forested areas. Travelling from Nairobi to Mombasa, the Lilac-breasted Roller can be seen nearly all the way, whereas the Rufous-crowned occurs only in the more arid parts of the bush. Some of the Lilac-breasted Rollers seen along the Kenya coast are of the Somali race, which is migratory, and has less lilac on the upper breast and throat than the nominate southern race.

Most rollers seem to be nomadic or migratory; and several tropical species migrate entirely within the tropics. For years I broke the monotony by counting the rollers of three species seen on journeys between Nairobi and Mombasa. Lilac-breasted Rollers occurred all the year round; but increased sharply in numbers in the long rains, from April onward Similarly, the Somalian race occurs in the arid Horn of Africa mainly from April–September, that is during the rains, though I have found them breeding in Ethiopia in March. In South Africa this roller is not said to be markedly migratory, though I suspect that there too it moves from one part of a vast area to another.

One might suppose that such movements, which seem to occur in response to weather conditions, (the onset of rains stimulating many rollers to migrate) would ultimately be controlled by food supply for the breeding season. However, I find this hard to believe for, taking one year with another, European Rollers outnumber by more than seven to one all other species in the East African thornbush during the European winter. Since they do not breed here, but certainly do eat the same sort of prey as other rollers, they must collectively consume several times the amount of food eaten by all the others. This implies that there can be no real limitation of food supply to prevent Lilac-breasted Rollers from breeding at any time of year they chose.

According to rather scanty records, Lilac-breasted Rollers breed in East Africa mainly in dry months, when insect life is less abundant. In Somalia and the Ethiopian bush, however, they definitely breed in the rains, and leave afterwards. Perhaps the optimum breeding time varies with the aridity of the country – in the wet in arid areas and in the dry in moister places; but we know too little about it.

Like their relatives, Lilac-breasted Rollers breed in holes in trees; lay white eggs, and being hole-nesters are rather hard to observe. Few nests are noticed till they contain large noisy young, when both parents go to and fro with food. Both sexes probably incubate; and certainly both feed young. From egg-laying to fledging of the young takes about six weeks; and the young depend on their parents for some time after they can fly. Probably rollers breed only once a year, if that, and may not breed if conditions are not right.

Lilac-breasted Rollers feed mainly on large insects, caught on the ground, or flying termites hawked on the wing in the rains. They also take small snakes and lizards, probably less often than does the larger Rufous-crowned Roller. Grasshoppers are very often caught as they flee the flames of a grass fire, which will certainly attract any rollers there are to an area. If it were not for other reasons undesirable to yield to pyromaniac tendencies one would be tempted to set fire to long grass, if only to watch the beauty of Lilac-breasted Rollers at close quarters as they sweep unconcerned through the smoke to snap up those fleeing grasshoppers.

Length sixteen inches, sexes alike

9 Schalow's Wheatear
Oenanthe lugens schalowi

Wheatears are not really typical birds of thick bush, but of open, stony or rocky downland, semi-desert, or rocky cliffs and valleys. This one, otherwise known as the Masai Chat since it is so common in parts of Masailand, frequents stony hillsides scattered with Acacia trees, and very commonly breeds in the deep gullies torn by watercourses in the old lakebed soils of the Kenya Rift Valley near Nairobi. Thus, it is locally found in the same sort of country as several other birds in this book, although other races are more birds of cliffs and rocky ravines in the highlands of Ethiopia, or rocky deserts in North Africa Schalow's Wheatear used to be regarded as a distinct species; but is now merged with the Abyssinian Black Wheatear and the North African Mourning Chat *Oenanthe lugens*.

The Masai Chat, like other wheatears, is a perky, cheerful, conspicuous bird which perches on large rocks or on stumps, and on being disturbed usually flies only a short way, exposing the conspicuous buff rump. As in most wheatears the sexes are different, the female being generally duller and lacking the grey cap of the male. They are resident throughout the year, a pair maintaining a territory and defending it vigorously during the breeding season.

They feed on insects, characteristically caught on the ground, or on the wing, by a short flight from a perch. The bird is always on the alert for possible prey, but often perches in the shade, when it is inconspicuous until it makes its swoop. In the breeding season they perch more out in the open and sing. No good description of the song in East Africa exists, though it may have been recorded on tape. In North Africa the song of the Mourning Chat is said to be variable, short and repetitive, or long and warbling, so you can take your choice. Alarmed, the bird utters a dull "chut-chut", very similar to the calls of many other chats and wheatears.

The male sings in the early rains, and breeding soon follows. He apparently has no very conspicuous form of display. Most nests in Kenya are found in March or April, and none are recorded in the latter half of the year when the short rains fall. This is curious, because the breeding season is short, like that of most small passerines, and there is no reason

Schalow's Wheatear

why they should not breed in the short as well as the long rains. However, more observation may prove that they do. Ethiopian birds breed also in the rains; while in North Africa the Mourning Chat breeds in spring like other Palearctic birds.

Nests may·be in holes in banks, recesses or holes in boulders, cliff ledges, or under a stone. In soft banks they are usually deeper in than in hard gravelly banks, which suggests that the bird may actually excavate its own tunnel. However, it is more likely that it uses or enlarges a ready made root or rodent hole. The actual nest is of grass, rootlets, etc, and is cup-shaped. The amount of material used will vary according to the site; and if they must, the parent birds will build up a sloping entrance with quite large stones till they have a level platform on which to build the nest proper.

The two or three eggs are blue or whitish, with a few black or brown markings, sometimes unmarked. No details are recorded on the share of the sexes in incubation; but as in the European Wheatear it is probably mainly or only the female that sits, the male feeding her with insects at intervals. However, he may sit for short periods. The eggs hatch in 13–14 days, which seems to be a common period for wheatears in general. The young when they hatch are dark brownish flesh, with sparse tufts of grey down.

When the young are small they are brooded by the female, but as they grow she emerges and assists the male in feeding them. They leave the nest in fourteen or fifteen days, according to Van Someren; but there are no more recent records. For some while the brood accompanies the parents and is fed in the neighbourhood of the nest; but they soon become independent.

This wheatear habitually nests in natural situations, but may also breed in houses, and would doubtless take to suitable nest boxes. Although it is very common in its local haunts, we still know too little about it. It should be quite easy for anyone who has one breeding in the house to fill in a few of the obvious gaps in our knowledge of this pleasant little bird.

Length six inches, male (lower) and female

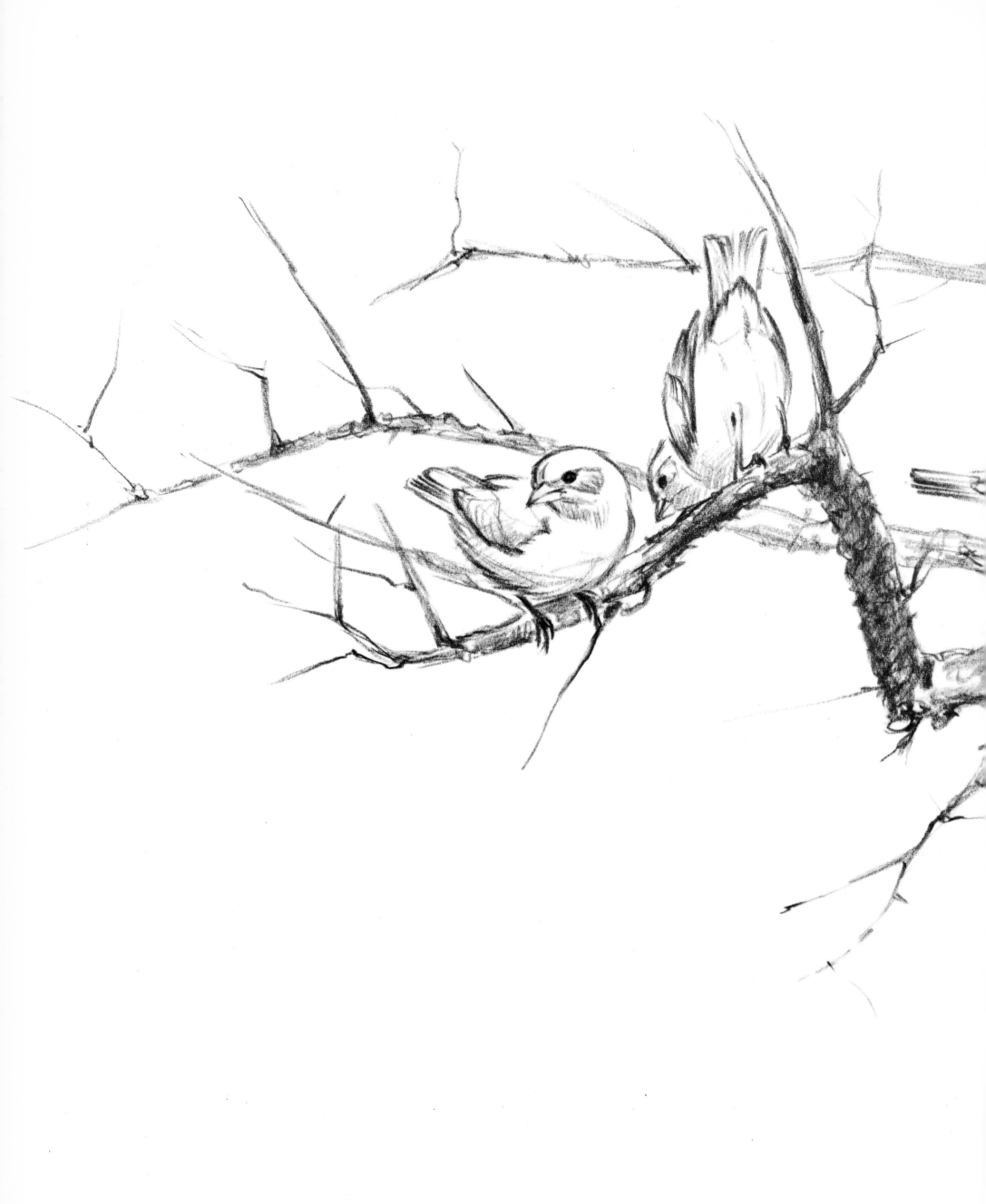

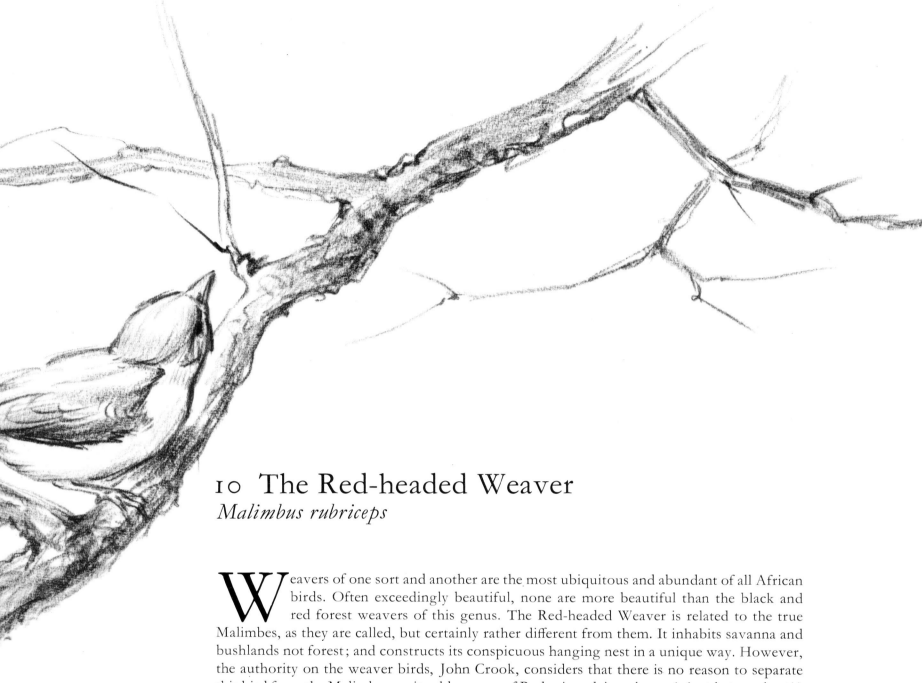

10 The Red-headed Weaver
Malimbus rubriceps

Weavers of one sort and another are the most ubiquitous and abundant of all African birds. Often exceedingly beautiful, none are more beautiful than the black and red forest weavers of this genus. The Red-headed Weaver is related to the true Malimbes, as they are called, but certainly rather different from them. It inhabits savanna and bushlands not forest; and constructs its conspicuous hanging nest in a unique way. However, the authority on the weaver birds, John Crook, considers that there is no reason to separate this bird from the Malimbes, so its older name of Red-winged Anaplectes (*Anaplectes melanotis*) has been abandoned.

The existing English name is highly confusing, for several weaver birds have red heads; and the female Red-headed Weaver does not. However, the earlier name was not much better; and it is also confusing to think of this bird as resembling any other Malimbe, all of which are entirely black and red birds of high forests. Fortunately, it is a highly distinctive bird in its own environment, and will not normally be mistaken for any other because of its unique mode of nesting and general habits. In the savanna and bushlands there is no other moderately large arboreal weaver with a red head. The Cardinal Quelea, which also has a red head, is more a bird of long grass country than of bushlands; and virtually every other male weaver bird of the bush is mainly bright yellow.

Red-headed Weavers live in pairs or small colonies, located in large trees, which continue to be occupied year after year for, to my knowledge, up to thirty years. They are found both in long-grass broad-leaved savanna and the moister parts of the thornbush, favouring areas with about thirty inches of rain a year, and not found much in arid thornbush proper, though they sometimes nest in big trees along watercourses here too. They are birds rather closely confined to a particular ecological type. If Red-headed Weavers are at all common one can say almost with certainty that the rainfall is around thirty inches a year, and the composition of the bush round about will confirm this. In my experience, they are commonest in Kenya where large *Terminalia* trees are scattered among *Combretum* woodland with long red oat or *Hyparrhenia* grass; but they also nest in acacias.

The Red-headed Weaver

There are normally five or six nests visible at any colony; but in East Africa there are seldom more than one or two males with attached females, often only one, responsible for all these nests. The reason lies in their unique construction of tough leaf petioles, tendrils, or springy green twigs, the finished structure lasting for up to three years, or six rainy seasons in the eastern Kenya savannas. The building material used is too stiff and springy to weave in the normal weaver-bird way; so the building male separates a little strip of the bark from the end of each green petiole and uses this to knot the new piece to the rest of the structure. This unique method of building results in a very strong and durable retort-shaped nest, hanging conspicuously from the tip of a bough. If you examine a group of these nests in the rains, a new one built that year is paler in colour and obviously fresher looking, the older ones dark and dry. When such colonies are found in the same trees for up to thirty years they must evidently be occupied in that time by a long succession of different males and females. They are almost as permanent as big eagles' nests.

This very unusual weaver is insectivorous, and consequently goes about in pairs or small parties. All the weavers that form into large flocks are seed eaters. Red-headed Weavers feed in the tops of trees more like tits or warblers than like true weaver birds, which collect seed from the ground. Even the female is fairly easily recognisable by her red bill; and she is likely to be soon joined by the distinctive male with his bright red head and breast. They are quiet birds, hardly uttering a sound except at the nest, even then only a soft clinking chatter quite unlike the continuous wheezy rasping notes of most of the common weavers.

Males normally build one or more new nests each rainy season; but breeding does not inevitably follow and may be controlled by the abundance or otherwise of the rains. The nest is a rough looking, open structure with a long spout, inside which the decorative male can be seen working. The female, when she arrives, lines the nest and lays in it; any nest in use can be recognised by the fact that it is lined and opaque, not transparent like an unlined structure. Two or three blue eggs are laid, sometimes with grey or brown spots, sometimes unmarked. Probably the female only incubates; but both sexes feed the young. In South Africa this species appears to be more polygamous than it is in East Africa, with colonies of up to forty nests in places.

The elaborate nests are probably useful for survival. Many weaver birds are severely harried by the African Harrier Hawk, which hangs on the nests and puts its head and bill in to eat the young. Apparently, the long spout of the Red-headed Weaver's nest helps to prevent such raiding, and also probably makes it more difficult for snakes to reach the entrance, at least unmolested. Again, I feel that the small number of occupied nests in each group, and the fact that a male may build a nest which is not used in a season to rear young, suggests that this is a relatively long-lived bird. Ringing studies could probably prove this point fairly easily, for these birds often nest near houses where they apparently feel that they obtain some protection from the proximity of human beings.

Length six inches, male and female (below)

11 The Red-and-Yellow Barbet
Trachyphonus erythrocephalus

Of all birds in the bush, this is one of the most bizarre, both in plumage and in its habits. It is a brilliant, but somehow not very beautiful creature, mainly yellow below and black with white spots above, with red cheeks adorned by a white crescent. Males have black crowns, females red, so that they are easy to distinguish.

Unlike most other barbets, which dig their own nest holes in dead trees as do woodpeckers, members of this genus either use a hole in a tree, or dig a hole in a bank, or even vertically, in flat ground. Although they are common, little has been learned about them. They present the usual difficulty of all birds that nest in holes in banks – the nest chamber itself is hard to see into to find out what goes on. In South Africa the related Levaillant's Barbet breeds in holes in trees in suburban gardens, so is easier to observe. Its behaviour probably gives some clues to that of its near relatives.

In the East African bush two species of these ground barbets occur, D'Arnaud's and the Red-and-yellow Barbet. Further north, in the sub-desert of Somalia and Ethiopia the Yellow-bellied Barbet also occurs. However, all three do not usually occur in exactly the same area, the Yellow-bellied preferring hotter, drier country. One knows that one or more species is there over the breakfast table, for they are very active early in the morning, and call loudly and repeatedly for the first hour or so of daylight. Thereafter they become less noisy, but call again in the evening as they go to roost.

During the day one may find them feeding quietly in any fruiting trees, several collecting together, especially in one of those fig trees with small round fruit, which they love. In their feeding habits they normally differ from other barbets, since they feed most often on the ground, underneath thick cover, and often near a termite mound. Probably, in such places they are feeding on termites and other insects which are their main food. They only take to fruit when it is available in quantity.

Most barbets are solitary, or live in pairs; and this is true even of the Levaillant's Barbet which breeds in holes in trees. However, the ground barbets, as we should call the

The Red-and-Yellow Barbet

Red-and-yellow, D'Arnaud's and the Yellow-bellied, live in small parties. They are slimmer, less stocky than the true barbets; and as befits an insectivorous bird have relatively slender bills. These bills are sharp and powerful; and I have been told by my Mbere eagle watchers that should a goat approach too close to a nesting hole the barbet will attack with such force that the goat's stomach may be pierced! I do not at present believe this story; but I have been told equally unlikely tales by these men, and found them to be true.

Pairs or parties of these barbets roost in holes in banks, and in the early morning emerge to feed and to call, establishing themselves in their territory. The call is a duet, or uttered by several birds together, perching in a bush and wagging their tails from side to side. It is almost impossible to describe adequately, and is well enough conveyed by Reg Moreau's "Lots o' burble". The duets of D'Arnaud's Barbet have been more fully described; and many hole nesting typical barbets call in duet, so that this habit is not unusual.

No full account of the nesting habits exist; but we know that Red-and-yellow Barbets normally breed in holes in banks or termite hills, occasionally in holes in trees. D'Arnaud's Barbet normally digs a hole in flat ground, so that these two related species do not compete for nesting space. The race inhabiting Somalia normally breeds in termite hills, apparently using the cylindrical tunnels made by the termites themselves. In East Africa the birds dig their own holes in banks, both sexes taking part. The burrows are about 18 inches deep, curving downward, with a circular chamber at the end. Thus, some members of this species work hard to make a home while others use ready made holes in termite mounds or trees.

In Kenya three or four eggs seem to be the normal clutch, but in Somalia five or six; like other barbet eggs they are white, but become stained with the earth on which they lie. More than one female may lay in the same nest; and up to ten eggs have been found in one hole. In fact, it is likely that this queer bird is sometimes a communal nester, with more than one male and female attached to the same nest hole. However, no good details have been published; and this is another bird that many campers in the bush could learn more about without too much trouble.

Breeding normally seems to take place in the rains, when insects and termites are abundant. In the early rains these barbets become more noisy, performing communal vocal displays. Eggs can be laid either in the short or long rains, and the young then emerge from the hole late in the rains or early in the dry season. Nothing is recorded on the share of the sexes in incubation, but when more than one bird lays in the same nest only one can incubate at the same time; so probably several may share this task. The incubation period, if similar to that of Levaillant's Barbet, is likely to be about two weeks, and the fledging period a month or more. Thus, if the best is to be made of the short rainy season and abundant food supply, the eggs must normally be laid early in the rains.

Few people feel like digging out occupied barbet burrows in banks, which must necessarily cause desertion of eggs or young. However, it is astonishing that more is not known of the general habits of this extraordinary and colourful bird, for many people must camp on river banks with the birds actually nesting in the vicinity, or at least going in and out of holes to roost. How many birds regularly use a hole? And is the fable about the barbets attacking goats based on fact – it easily could be for many salt-licks are in river banks. Once again, there is plenty left to learn.

Length nine inches, male and female (with black cap)

12 The Paradise Whydah
Vidua paradisea

The first time I ever saw a male Paradise Whydah in full livery, in a village in Nigeria, I was struck dumb with astonishment, only to be rudely distracted by my servant who, playing with my shotgun, almost blew his head off. The bang frightened the bird away and it was the only one I ever saw in Nigeria, for I lived in long grass savanna too far south for Paradise Whydahs to be abundant. However, I came across them again in my first rainy season in Kenya, and found them as spectacular and surprising as I remembered from that first encounter.

Paradise Whydahs used to be placed in a separate genus *Steganura* because of their gigantic and unlikely-looking tails. The male in full breeding dress would qualify for the title of Africa's most spectacular if not most beautiful small bird (for my money many sunbirds would beat him). The black back, wings, and face contrast strongly with a yellow nape, a rufous breast, and white belly, at the rear end of which grows the astonishing tail. This too is black, finely barred with paler brown, and the vanes of the central feathers stand vertically, like a coxcomb, broad and tipped with long bare shafts. The outer feathers are up to thirteen inches long, broad and tapering, again with the vanes vertical, but hanging down below the central coxcomb feathers. On the ground the tail is clearly an inconvenience, and likely to become badly worn after a time; but its main function is in the air.

The male Paradise Whydah in song-flight flies high above the bush, undulating jerkily as he alternately flaps and rests his wings, with the central tail feathers elevated well above the trailing outer feathers, so that the whole assembly, as one might call it, looks like a huge broad tail projected by a small forward engine. The song is not really audible; but the skipping aerial display is so eye-catching that no female within half a mile could fail to see it if she was in receptive mood. Locating a female, the male drops and hovers over her, bobbing up and down with slow wing beats, each beat jerking his magnificent tail. In this display there are elements both of the vertical dancing of the Pin-tailed Whydah, and of the almost equally spectacular curving aerial displays of unrelated Widow-birds of the genus *Euplectes*, especially

The Paradise Whydah

the almost equally unbelievable Sakabula or Long-tailed Widow-bird. All these, incidentally, used to be called Whydahs; but this name should properly only be applied to the long tailed parasitic Estrildine weavers of the genus *Vidua*. The name originally comes from the West African town, Widah.

There are actually at least two species of Paradise Whydahs, sometimes called the Broad-tailed and the Narrow-tailed. The outer tail feathers of the Broad-tailed are shorter and broader than in the commoner Paradise Whydah, and the central coxcomb feathers are smaller. The basic display pattern, however, is the same in both species; but in East Africa the Broad-tailed is much less numerous than the normal long Narrow-tailed species. Since both occur in the same areas they are distinct species, and not mere races. Of the two, the typical Paradise Whydah with the long sabre-like outer tail feathers is the more spectacular; but each can be recognised in song flight with the naked eye at a quarter of a mile or more. It is the astonishing tail one sees dancing across the sky.

All these long-tailed Whydahs are parasitic on other small Estrildine weaver birds, and their relations with their hosts have been obscure in the wild state. They have been better studied in aviaries in captivity, and here it has been proven that the two Paradise Whydahs are distinct species because they only parasitise different hosts. All Paradise Whydahs parasitise Melba Finches and Pytilias (genus *Pytilia*); but the common Paradise Whydah parasitises the Melba Finch *Pytilia melba* and the Broad-tailed the Golden-backed Pytilia *P. afra*.

In South and East Africa only these two species of Pytilias occur, so there are two clear species of Paradise Whydahs. In West Africa, however, the Red and Yellow-winged Pytilias also occur in longer grass country. These are parasitised by Paradise Whydahs with broader, shorter outer tail feathers, now placed in the Broad-tailed group, though the Togoland version has nearly as long a tail as the typical Paradise Whydah of East Africa. It may well prove, in time, that the bird from which I was distracted when my servant nearly blew off his head was a different species to the one I saw years later in eastern Kenya. Quite possibly, each of four species of Pytilia hosts its own species of Paradise Whydah.

Female Paradise Whydahs are dull and stripey, like little sparrows; and after the breeding season the males drop their astonishing plumes and moult into dull colours like the females and young. They then associate with other small Estrildine weavers, feeding in mixed flocks on the ground. Flocks of almost pure males, still with tails, form towards the end of the rains, and such a flock is a truly astonishing sight when one has the luck to meet it. One male is unlikely enough; ten perched on a bare tree top make one whistle.

Since Pytilias are shy retiring little birds of thick bush the parasitic habits of Paradise Whydahs have not been much studied in the wild state. However, it is known that the young Paradise Whydahs are willingly fed by their unsuspecting hosts because they have very similar mouth markings. The eggs are apparently rather larger than those of the Pytilia; but also white. Anyone who finds a Pytilia nest with such an egg in it could watch it with advantage, and so add to our knowledge of this astonishing and spectacular bird.

Length, male fifteen to sixteen inches, female five inches. Courtesy, John G. Tremlett, Esq., Kenya

13 The Red-backed Scrub Robin
Cercotrichas leucophrys

Thus far we have been talking only about birds that are quite easy to see; but some of the bush birds are harder to find, and Scrub Robins and Morning Warblers are among them. They skulk in thickets for the most part, emerging little into the open, and betraying their presence mainly by song in the rains. Careful watching at the right time of year is usually needed to get a good view of a Scrub Robin; but when it does appear in an open place it is rewarding, with nicely variegated plumage, dark spots on a white breast, and a characteristic bright rufous rump.

The rufous rump used to place this bird, with several other species known as Scrub Robins, in a convenient genus *Erythropygia* – meaning red-rumped. Then, if one knew a little dog latin, one knew where one was. Nowadays, systematists bring down on their heads the curses of ordinary bird watchers by lumping genera; and this one has recently been merged in *Cercotrichas*, a genus which in Africa formerly only included the Black Bush-robin, *Cercotrichas podobe*, an almost entirely black species frequenting deserts and sub-deserts, and totally different in appearance to the rather bright and variegated Scrub Robins formerly included in *Erythropygia*. Systematists can no doubt find good anatomical or other reasons for this; but such changes are a nuisance to ordinary people, and are part of the reason why so many turn to even more confusing English or vernacular names, because no two books agree as to the proper scientific name. What we all used to know as the White-winged Scrub-robin *E. leucoptera* has now also been merged with this species, which used to be called *E. zambesiana*; and both have been merged with the White-browed Scrub Robin *E. leucophrys*.

Anyway, if these systematic difficulties are accepted, then this bird occurs all through the thornbush and dry savannas from Eritrea and the Sudan to Malawi and South Africa. If one can overcome, by the necessary mental effort, the vagaries of systematists (which may change again in a few years) it is a common but rather unobtrusive bird of thickets in thornbush and savanna throughout this wide range. In some places it becomes more confiding, frequenting gardens and the vicinity of houses; but it is generally rather hard to see, feeding

The Red-backed Scrub Robin

low in bushes, and when approached, flitting across a space to the next cover a few feet above the ground. At intervals, it fans its tail jerkily; and when singing raises it right above the back and fans it. There is little doubt that the red rump is used in display, both nuptial and threat.

Throughout its East African range this bird breeds in the rains, and is then easier to see. The male sings in the early morning from the top of or within a bush. His song is not distinguished, but is pleasant, a short series of whistled notes. Singing, he droops his wings, and raises and jerks his tail, sometimes bringing it so far forward that it almost touches his head. Displaying to his mate, he runs along a branch, with his wings drooped, head bowed, and raised tail, all actions which display his conspicuous markings. The sexes are alike; but we assume it is only the male who performs these nuptial antics.

Nests are always close to the ground in thick cover, often on a base of growing grass, or in the bottom of a thick bush. The exterior is roughly constructed of grass and small twigs, but in the centre is a neat cup of finer materials, hair being used for lining when available – as it very often is when game or cattle are plentiful. Both in Kenya and South Africa two or three eggs are laid, white, usually evenly freckled with dark brown, but sometimes with a ring of markings round the broad end.

Only the female sits as far as known; but the male may do so, and the sexes can hardly be distinguished. The eggs hatch in twelve days, and are fed mainly on insects, including caterpillars, small moths, beetles and grubs but also some spiders, small millipedes etc. The fledging period is not recorded but is probably short, not more than two weeks, so that the whole breeding season can be accomplished in little over a month. This is a necessary feature to take advantage of the short period when insect food is abundant in the rains. In Kenya at least this Scrub Robin breeds in both the long and short rains, but more often in the long rains. Late long rains broods may be genuine seconds, but more likely repeats after loss of the first.

The parents are tame and easily photographed when they are feeding young; and since they approach the nest by regular routes, including perches on stones or conspicuous twigs, the fact that the nest is in thick cover need not deter anyone. At each staging point they raise the tail as they alight, with a more exaggerated jerk right over the back when they reach the nest itself.

Once the rains are over Scrub Robins become harder to find again, though they have actually increased in number because of the fledged broods. However, a little patience, in the early morning or evening, will usually reveal them, though they may keep more to the base of thick cover and scarcely sing, except a brief phrase or two at dawn. They are typical of the way abundant life retreats in the bush in the hard times; but they are there and reappear in cheerful song as soon as the rains come again.

Length six inches, sexes alike. Courtesy, Mr. and Mrs. C. P. Luxmoore, England

14 The Beautiful Sunbird
Nectarinia pulchella

Male sunbirds are mostly exquisite little gems; and when one has to be singled out as specially beautiful then it's a gem indeed. Metallic golden-green, long-tailed, graceful, and with a splash of bright red in the middle of a yellow cummerbund the male Beautiful Sunbird is certainly hard to beat. The female is, like most female sunbirds, dull and short-tailed.

Fortunately, there is no difficulty in seeing this sunbird, for it is common and widespread over a huge tract of bush from West Africa to Ethiopia and Central Tanzania. In North Eastern Kenya and Tanzania it is replaced by a very similar species, unromantically named the Smaller Black-bellied Sunbird, which differs only in that the male has an orange-red, not bright red chest. Females would be practically indistinguishable; and one would have thought that if systematists *must* lump species together they might have done it here, for the habits of the two do not differ appreciably and their ranges do not seem to overlap.

Sunbirds feed a lot on nectar; and one wonders where on earth nectar is to be found in dry thornbush. The answer is that there are plenty of succulents which produce nectar, such as the very abundant aloes; and that many of the bush trees are also festooned with parasitic plants of the mistletoe family which, being parasites, do not have to produce many leaves but can flower and fruit profusely. These plants are of great value to sunbirds for nectar and also, later on when in fruit, to small barbets, which spread them from tree to tree by wiping their beaks to rid them of the sticky seeds. When aloes are not in flower these mistletoe plants often are; and any tree which is parasitised will inevitably be visited by sunbirds. In fact, if a sunbird is flitting about in the crown of the flat-topped acacia under which you rest, the odds are that it is seeking the flowers of the mistletoe plants, not of the acacia itself.

Nectar food is supplemented with small insects, very often caught on the wing. Sunbirds are often likened to the New World humming-birds, but they are not closely related, are usually much bigger, and feed a great deal on insects besides nectar. Some are, in fact, more insectivorous than nectar eaters. Beautiful Sunbirds take many small insects attracted to

The Beautiful Sunbird

flowers; and one wonders which came first, nectar-sipping or insect eating. Possibly, small insectivorous ancestral sunbirds found that insects were abundant near flowers; then took to drinking nectar themselves; and later developed the specialised long curved bills necessary to reach into or puncture the longer tubular flowers, while retaining the ability to catch insects at will. Without insects, bush-loving sunbirds such as this one would find it hard to subsist year round on nectar.

Male sunbirds are favourites of photographers, and many a colour photograph competition has been won by setting up a hide near an aloe in flower. The sunbird is inevitably attracted; and the photograph is taken. Hardly anyone bothers with the poor, dull female; but she is the one who builds the nest and does most of the actual work of rearing the brood. I cannot find any detail recorded of the breeding habits of the Beautiful Sunbird, so we must assume they resemble those of other sunbirds.

Males sing from conspicuous perches, and are aggressively territorial to other males of their species, or even others. They display to and chivvy the females from place to place, but do little else. They toil not, neither do they spin, but they are active in defence of the nesting site from such very much larger birds as shrikes, which could eat the eggs or young; so they do perform a useful function in the breeding season. They accompany the female to and fro when she starts to build the nest, but usually take no part in building or incubation, though they may feed her during building and on the nest, and later share in feeding the young. Apparently, smaller, duller, short-tailed male sunbirds take more part in nesting duties than do the exceptionally beautiful long-tailed species. Whether this is true of the Beautiful Sunbird remains to be recorded; once again, there is plenty left to learn.

All sunbirds make nests that are works of art, pendent from the tip of a twig, or under a leaf. Cobwebs are used as suspension and binding material; and a female seen collecting cobwebs from among bark is almost certainly building. A cup is then fashioned of grass or other fine material, and this is usually later lined with plant down, occasionally feathers. The most beautiful nest I ever saw was a Beautiful Sunbird's nest at Lake Hannington; this particular female had lined it softly with the exquisite pink feathers of flamingoes. The outside is usually adorned, or rather camouflaged with bits of lichen, dead leaves, or seed pods, so that the nest resembles a mass of hanging debris. They are not usually high up, but in situations where snakes find it hard to reach them, while the aggressive male drives off other intruders.

Sunbirds often take weeks to build their nests, and having built them, may not lay that year; if so, they build a new nest next season, often near the old one. They lay only one or two eggs, the Beautiful Sunbird usually two, less often one. These are white, spotted with grey and brown; and in species which have been watched hatch in about fourteen days. The female normally incubates alone; her long curved beak can usually be seen protruding from the nest entrance. She sits close, but leaves to feed from time to time. When the young hatch they are at first brooded by the female, but quite soon left alone while she and the male bring insect food. Often the male accompanies the feeding female, singing uselessly if decoratively, while she does the actual work. The young leave the nest in sixteen or seventeen days in large species, and are always dull like the female at first. Later, the young male begins to don the glorious plumage of his male parent. It seems odd to suggest that such a small bird could be quite long-lived; but the small clutch and irregular breeding of sunbirds suggests that this is so.

Length, male six inches, female four and a half inches

15 The Blackhead Plover

Vanellus tectus

One associates plovers with watersides, marshes, at least open grassy plains and meadows, not with arid thornbush. Yet here is one which is otherwise a perfectly typical member of the Lapwing group, but which is found in thornbush and sandy plains, often far from water and clearly independent of it. In some of its wide African range it is found in open patches among the bush, or open plains; but in East Africa may occur in bush so dense that one cannot see thirty yards.

Among an ornamental and graceful group this is one of the prettiest and neatest, with a black crested head, red legs, red wattles in front of the eye, and a deep black V on the chest encircling a white shirt front and splitting the brown breast like a necklace. Above, it is mainly dull brown, so that the plover at rest is not obvious to a questing hawk or eagle. The striking black and white front, and the pied wings when opened are probably used in nuptial or aggressive display, as they are in several related species. Large animals such as warthogs, maybe even elephants, can be scared away by the sudden exposure of black and white wings, coupled with a bold demeanour and loud shrill calls.

Ordinarily, Blackhead Plovers are stealthy, unobtrusive creatures. Not found every-where in the bush – for instance there is one small group on the Njemps flats of Baringo district and none in most of the area – they are easily overlooked since they are often inactive by day. As you approach they will walk stealthily away; and unless you happen to be looking in that direction you will miss them. Several pairs may be found close together; and when not breeding they form into small flocks, but never collect in big flocks like some other lap-wings. Only when they have young are they likely to be both noisy and obvious.

Ordinarily silent, when they take wing or are courting they utter shrill, lilting calls, resembling those of the Crowned and Spurwing Plovers, but sharper, more piercing. At night, when camped in their haunts, especially in the rains when they think of breeding, one may hear them passing over against the stars, calling as they go. To me the nightly revels of plovers and other waders have been a lifelong pleasure; and to hear the Blackhead Plovers courting while

The Blackhead Plover

the great thunderheads flicker with internal fire all around the horizon in the otherwise black and silent bush puts me in mind of winter nights on Scottish saltings where the Lapwings and Oystercatchers keep the solitary wildfowler company.

Blackhead Plovers are apparently active mainly at night, like the bush-dwelling coursers. One observer in Gambia said that they seemed by day sluggish and inactive, like someone who has spent a wakeful night. They are said to feed on insects and small molluscs, picked up on the ground. Like other such plovers, when feeding they run a few steps, pause, appear to listen, and then bend to pick up something small, Their short bills are not suited to probing in soil; and anyway the earth in most of their haunts is baked brick-hard for much of the year. They may well feed all night, in moonlight at least, and by day are most likely to be found resting quietly in the shade.

They are generally nomadic or migratory, but their movements are a mystery. In Northern Nigeria they leave the more southern parts of their range in the height of the rains, and no one knows where they go, probably further north, to drier areas, like many other birds. In East Africa where the rains are irregular in the dry bush country they may not move so far or so regularly as in West Africa.

Like other plovers they nest on the ground. In East Africa most records are for the latter part of the rains, in April and May in north-east Kenya, occasionally later, in July or September. In Ethiopia I have found nests in March, following early rains in the Awash Valley. In Uganda they nest December to March, in June and September; in Northern Nigeria in November. Possibly the breeding season depends on the intensity of the rainfall, in the rains in really dry areas, but in the dry season or late rains in areas of heavier rainfall.

Unlike other such plovers, however, the Blackhead Plover normally lays only one or two eggs; I can find a record of only one clutch of three. Possibly this small clutch, in contrast to the 3–4 normally laid by, for instance the Blacksmith, Crowned and Spurwing Plovers in East Africa is an adaptation to an arid habitat. It may just be impossible to rear large broods in such areas. Parents are normally seen accompanied by only one or two downy young, and these young stay with them till they can fly. All then form into small flocks, and perhaps migrate, in the non-breeding seasons.

The eggs are beautifully camouflaged, stone-colour marked with black. The nests are right in the blaze of the sun, on open ground. In such places the ground temperature can be such as to scorch a bare foot; and the plover combats it by half burying the eggs in small clods of earth, or stones. This is also done by, for instance Spurwing and Blacksmith Plovers. Both sexes incubate in turn; but by day the blazing heat makes true incubation unnecessary, and the plover just stands over the eggs, gaping, shading them from the sun. Probably the eggs are daily buried and unburied, according to the temperature, the attendant bird lifting each little separate clod and placing it carefully around the egg. In such marvellous ways birds adapt to the sometimes cruel habitats they live in; and this graceful plover, which one would think more fitted to watersides, manages to live in near desert.

Length ten inches, sexes alike

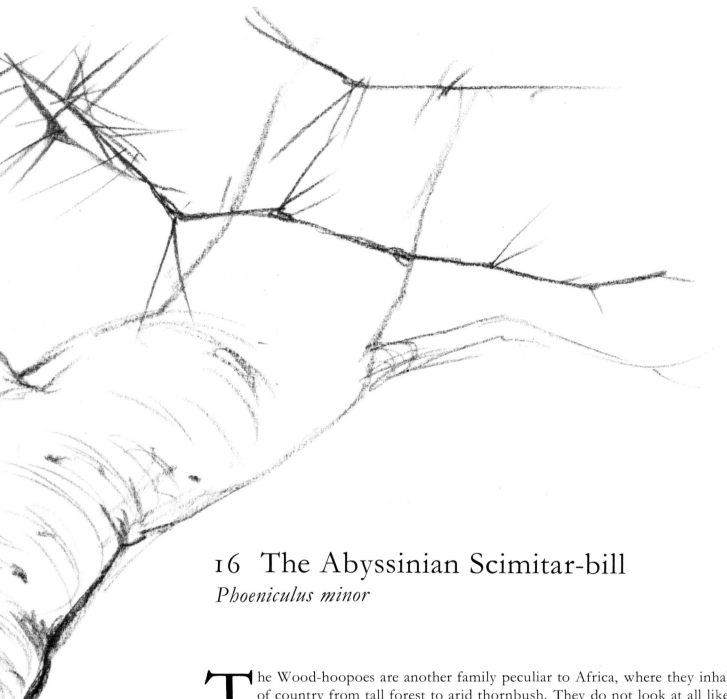

16 The Abyssinian Scimitar-bill
Phoeniculus minor

The Wood-hoopoes are another family peculiar to Africa, where they inhabit all types of country from tall forest to arid thornbush. They do not look at all like the typical orange and black barred crested hoopoes; but are chiefly glossy dark birds, that go about in small parties and are often very noisy. The Abyssinian Scimitar-bill is the smallest of the lot; and not very easy to see for it goes about its business quietly, and its call is low and musical, unlike the harsh cackle of the larger species. It also differs from most others in having no white spots on the relatively short tail; and from its nearest relative the Scimitar-bill by having a bright yellow bill. It is actually a very beautiful little bird, shining glossy blue in sunlight; but none too easy to keep in view as it flits from tree to tree.

Like other wood-hoopoes it lives in small parties, sometimes in pairs, or singly. It is restless, ever searching through the leafy tops of acacias, and moving on rapidly from one tree to another. One usually sees no more than four together; and when one flies, with dipping undulating flight from one tree to the next the others soon follow. Young birds can be distinguished from their parents by their dusky bills; and from the commoner Black-billed Scimitar-bill by the lack of white spots in the tail.

One thinks of a scimitar as a sharp, curved cutting sword; but in this case it is only the curve that gives the name. The instrument is actually a delicate hooked probe, evolved to catch the small insects on which the Scimitar-bills feed. It works equally well for poking around the globose flowers of acacias or probing tiny crannies in bark; but its most specialised application is really neat.

In much of Africa black clay plains are covered with a particular acacia known as whistling thorn (*Acacia drepanolobium*). In itself, this is an astonishing tree, for it produces large bulbous hollow growths at the base of its long paired thorns. At one time, these were thought to be galls produced by the bite of an insect; but recent research at Dakar, and later in Strasbourg has shown that the tree still produces the galls even when there could not possibly be any insects to sting it. It is a beautiful method of defence for the tree, for the

The Abyssinian Scimitar-bill

galls become inhabited by ants of the genus *Crematogaster*, which swarm out when the tree is shaken. Giraffes, which nibble the leaves of acacias, don't seem to mind the ants; but elephants, which could easily smash the whole trees, apparently never touch the whistling thorn. The tree is one of the most horrid of all acacias to climb, for not only are the thorns fierce, but the swarms of ants are almost unbearable.

Anyway, the ants make their nests in the hollow galls or bulbs. They come and go through a little round hole, about two millimetres across or less; it is these holes which, in a wind, produce the hollow moaning or whistling that gives the tree its common name. One would think the ants and their eggs fairly safe inside such a stronghold, hard, and immune even to elephants. However, they aren't, for the curved probe of the Scimitar-bill is just the thing for pushing into that little hole and exploring the whole interior. Probably the Scimitar-bill has a long tongue which it can use to explore inside; but no one can see quite what happens. However, it is quite certain that both species of Scimitar-bills, the Abyssinian more often, systematically work along the branches of whistling thorns probing each gall in turn, and getting something from within. Whatever they take is always very small, for one never sees them obviously swallow anything.

Scimitar-bills are not confined to where the whistling thorn grows, they probably also probe the smaller galls of some other species of acacias, and can manage very well when there are no gall-acacias at all. However, I have found them commoner among whistling thorn than anywhere else. They are true birds of the dry acacia woodlands and bush, not found anywhere in high rainfall, and rare where broad-leaved trees mix with acacias. They never seem to move much; once you have located their haunts the same family party will probably pass close by each day on their rounds. The Abyssinian Scimitar-bill appears much more restricted to acacia country than the rather larger Black-billed Scimitar-bill.

Little is known about their nesting habits; but they breed in holes in trees, usually much too small to put a hand inside to see what's there, and in a gnarly trunk where one can't even probe with any surety of reaching the eggs. One must cut the tree open to find out; and that means desertion, so none but egg-collectors do it. What little is known suggests that like other insectivorous birds they breed in the rains; but there are plenty of ants in ant-gall acacias all the year round so this may not always be so. They lay two or three blue eggs; but almost nothing is known about their breeding cycle.

Other, larger wood-hoopoes go about in bigger parties of up to ten or more; and in the common Green Wood-hoopoe, well named Kakelaar from its raucous cackle, probably many members of the group feed the young of one pair in the nesthole. While no one knows, it seems unlikely that this occurs in the Abyssinian Scimitar-bill, which often lives in pairs. However, should you see one nesting, watch it; its pretty certain that in an hour or two you can record something quite new.

Length nine inches, male (nearest) and female

17 The Yellow-billed Hornbill
Tockus flavirostris

Of all the bush hornbills the Yellow-billed is both one of the most widespread, and also the handsomest. It is bigger than the Red-billed, Von der Decken's, or Jackson's; and both the latter have a more restricted range. The Yellow-billed Hornbill does not extend to West Africa, but is a common and characteristic bush bird from Somalia and the Sudan to South Africa. In South Africa it is relatively commoner than in East Africa, perhaps because Von der Decken's and Jackson's Hornbills do not occur there.

All these small bush hornbills have rather similar habits. They are to some extent ecologically separated; that is, when several species occur together in one country, one prefers one sort of bush and another different vegetation. Thus, the Red-billed Hornbill is decidedly more catholic in its tastes than the Yellow-billed, which sticks to the thornbush proper. Like others, it catches most of its food on the ground; and indeed spends more time hopping about on the ground than in trees when feeding. When catching flying termites as they emerge in swarms with the onset of the rains, however, the Yellow-billed Hornbill is capable of agile feats of flight.

Yellow-billed Hornbills normally live in pairs or small parties. They can instantly be recognised from all others by the bright yellow bill, which is smaller in the female than in the male. Young have a duller coloured bill; but are usually seen with their parents in a family party. The wings are spotted with white, and there are two conspicuous white bars across the tail, excepting the central deck feathers. When the hornbill turns its head to look at you its eye is yellow and clever-looking. One feels that although this bird may look a bit of a fool it is not.

Any hornbill's bill, like that of a toucan, looks unwieldy, but in fact is not. That of the Yellow-billed Hornbill is a nicely balanced blade-shaped structure, very light, useful not only for grasping insects and fruits, but as a trowel when nesting. Insects are picked up in the tip of the bill, crushed, and rapidly swallowed with a backward toss of the head. If any fruits are taken the hornbill rolls them between the mandibles to place them in the right position before giving the backward jerk that sends them into its gullet.

The Yellow-billed Hornbill

In the dry season Yellow-billed Hornbills feed most in early morning and evening, and often rest in the shade by day. They move over quite a large area each day; and if one is resting under a baobab tree at lunchtime it is likely that a hornbill will arrive, work its way through the tree branches, and move on after a few minutes. Many may congregate where there is a ready supply of suitable insect food, whether flying termites or grasshoppers. They become more active during the rains, and now the males perform their absurd displays, bobbing up and down with flapping wings and uttering deep baritone, sobbing or tooting calls. It seems ridiculous to us; but is doubtless satisfying to female hornbills.

The nesting habits of hornbills have fascinated many observers, and those of all bush hornbills of the genus *Tockus*, the Yellow-billed included, are much the same. A hole in a tree is chosen, often one with a large hollow area above into which female or young can escape if the nest is attacked. The pair first start to plaster the nesting hole entrance with mud, and then the female enters and seals herself in with her own droppings. Far from being incarcerated therein by an oppressive mate, she retreats to relative safety and locks herself in, leaving him to do all the work of feeding her, and later the whole brood. If any danger from predators has to be faced it is the male who faces it; no doubt right and proper too.

Once inside, the female lays two to four white or whitish eggs. She moults all her quills at once and her body feathers by degrees, becoming flightless. If the male were killed at this stage she would be in great difficulties, but he seldom is killed. She receives prey through the narrow slit, just wide enough to take the blade-shaped bill. He feeds her throughout the incubation period and during the first part of the fledging period, when he must also feed the young. Food remains and the droppings of the small young are thrown out of the nest slit, so that the nest is kept clean.

After about six to seven weeks when the young are part-grown, the female emerges, breaking open the nest entrance. She has now grown new feathers, but looks draggled and worn. The young at once seal themselves in again, using their own droppings. They do not make as neat a job of it as the adults, but the result is effective. They have powerful legs, but their wings and feathers are scarcely developed. Their strong legs not only enable them to clamber up the inside of the chamber to escape possible enemies, but also assist in nest sanitation. The female is no longer there to help in throwing out droppings, so they back up to the nest entrance and forcibly defaecate out of it. They throw out food remains with their beaks.

The female can now assist the male in feeding the young. In some large forest hornbills the male must continue to feed female and young for the entire fledging period, but in these bush species the short period of abundant food during the rains probably necessitates earlier emergence by the female. The young, in turn, break their way out of the nest hole when their feathers are grown; and thereafter accompany their parents and soon learn to catch insect food for themselves.

There is no doubt that this unusual method of nesting reduces predation. Very few hornbill nests suffer from predators whereas those of rollers, starlings, hoopoes and others are frequently robbed. The males seem to be able also to avoid being killed, though they are occasionally taken by several species of eagles. Again, this is an essential feature of hornbill biology – the male simply must survive, at least till the female emerges. In such areas as Tsavo, elephants are one of the main threats to hornbills because they smash most of the nesting trees. But the bush habitat is vast, and elephants are reduced in most of it, so that the hornbills will keep going for a long time yet.

Length seventeen to twenty inches, male

18 The Nubian Woodpecker
Campethera nubica

In Africa as a whole woodpeckers are often unaccountably scarce. They are not seen everywhere, as they are among North American woodlands; nor are they as abundant and conspicuous as they are in very similar open jungles of India. There are many species; but they are without exception medium-sized or small. None is like the magnificent crow-sized Black Woodpeckers of Europe, or the Pileated Woodpeckers of America. The largest African woodpecker, the Bearded, is not nearly as big as a European Green Woodpecker; and most are much smaller. This relative absence of woodpeckers is strange, because if there is one thing which is plentiful it is dead wood and, one assumes, grubs in it, which many different sorts of woodpeckers should utilise. Opposite my house there is a forest with plenty of dead wood; yet I have only seen one woodpecker – a Bearded – in it in fifteen years.

The Nubian Woodpecker is one of the larger African species and also one of the most obvious. Its presence becomes known immediately through its loud ringing cry, "keeet-keeet-keet-keet-keet" repeated five or six times, and audible half a mile away at least. Having heard the cry, an approach through the bush will soon locate the bird itself, by its tap-tap-tapping on a branch as it searches for food. They are not shy, but like most woodpeckers will creep round to and up the back of a branch if one approaches too close. Pressed, they will fly from one tree to the next with a typical undulating woodpecker flight.

They are to be found in any sort of acacia woodland and thornbush from the Sudan south to Malawi, but where the bush is low and thorny will usually be seen in the lines of big flat-topped acacias along watercourses. They also occur in more luxuriant broad-leaved woodland, sometimes even in the fringes of forests. Personally, I find woodpeckers among the hardest species to identify with certainty; but in East Africa a good motto is "when in doubt say Nubian". It is by far the most generally distributed of all East African species except the much smaller Cardinal Woodpecker; and is immediately distinguished from the more widespread Grey Woodpecker by its spotted and barred, not plain golden back.

The Nubian Woodpecker

There are generally a pair together; and males are easily distinguished from females by their red crowns, and bright red moustaches. Females have dark, spotted crowns, and no moustache. Young resemble the female, but young males soon develop red crown feathers. They should not, actually, be easily confused with other woodpeckers occurring in the same habitat; but I always have to look twice if they keep silent.

Very little detail seems to be known about the habits of any African woodpeckers, but they resemble others in many ways. They make their own nest holes in rotten stumps, the Nubian Woodpecker often choosing the dead stub of an acacia from four to thirty feet above ground. The nest chamber is nicely made, deep and cylindrical, too deep for the eggs to be felt with the tip of one's fingers, so that to find out the contents one needs a special scoop, a small mirror and torch, or must destroy the nest to take the eggs. The few people who have actually done this report that there are two to three white eggs, resembling those of other woodpeckers. The hole apparently takes about a month to dig, and young may be found in it six weeks after starting. Both parents are then seen visiting the hole with food; but they are cautious and best observed from some distance away or in concealment.

I fancy that this woodpecker drums in display, because I have heard the characteristic loud drumming of woodpeckers in its haunts. However, I have not certainly been able to identify the drummer, which might also have been the Bearded Woodpecker – which certainly does drum. The drumming of woodpeckers is often a substitute for loud calling; and since loud calling is what draws attention to the Nubian Woodpecker nine times out of ten it may not after all drum. However, this illustrates how little we know. Anyone – myself included – may with advantage watch a Nubian Woodpecker for an hour and record exactly what it does and how it forages, by tapping, digging, probing or otherwise.

These woodpeckers seem to breed both in the dry and in the wet season; and since there is no reason why insects living in dead stumps should be markedly more abundant in one than the other this is understandable. Once the young have left the hole for their first flight they probably return to it to roost; and may be seen with their parents in small foraging parties until they become independent.

Woodpeckers all over Africa are victimised by honeyguides. The young honeyguide, hatched in the bottom of a dark barbet or woodpecker's hole, cannot lift its nest mates to the entrance as a young cuckoo can throw them out of a shallow nest. It disposes of them in an even more malevolent way, since it is hatched with a pair of sharp hooks on its mandibles, with which it blindly mauls its nest-mates till they die, or perhaps punctures eggs. I have watched Nubian Woodpeckers trying to drive away both Scaly-throated and Lesser Honeyguides from their nest-hole. But the honeyguides are very persistent, quiet, and clever; and the odds are that they will catch the woodpecker unawares and lay an egg in the hole, so dooming the woodpecker's own brood. However, the Nubian Woodpecker always is far more abundant than any honeyguide, so evidently as in cuckoos both have struck the balance necessary for survival.

Length seven inches, male and female (above)

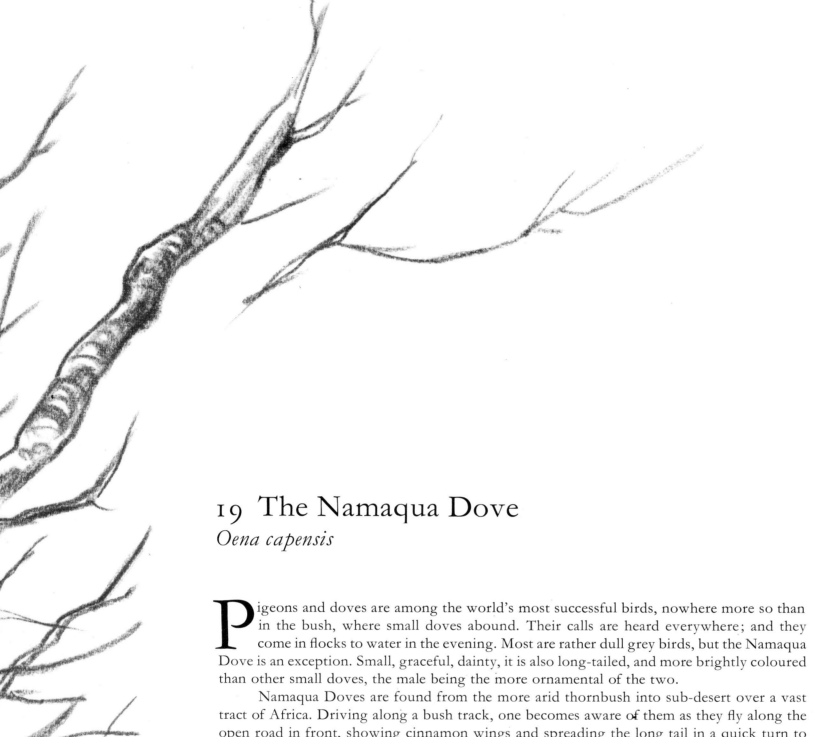

19 The Namaqua Dove
Oena capensis

Pigeons and doves are among the world's most successful birds, nowhere more so than in the bush, where small doves abound. Their calls are heard everywhere; and they come in flocks to water in the evening. Most are rather dull grey birds, but the Namaqua Dove is an exception. Small, graceful, dainty, it is also long-tailed, and more brightly coloured than other small doves, the male being the more ornamental of the two.

Namaqua Doves are found from the more arid thornbush into sub-desert over a vast tract of Africa. Driving along a bush track, one becomes aware of them as they fly along the open road in front, showing cinnamon wings and spreading the long tail in a quick turn to slip through an opening at the side of the track. They travel fast and direct, with typical dove-like flight, but seldom fly above the level of bushes or low trees. In more arid thornbush they are among the most abundant doves, probably the commonest small species; but they disappear or are scarce in long grass country with broad-leaved trees. Normally alone or in pairs, they also often form into loose flocks with other species of doves.

They feed on the ground, walking slowly and rather pompously, picking up seeds. If they come out into the open they are alert and watchful, flashing into flight if the shadow of a bird of prey passes over, soon to relax and feed again once it has gone. Many plants of the desert and sub-desert are annuals, which produce great quantities of seeds in relation to their total bulk. Thus, seed-eating birds such as doves can usually find plenty to eat, even in a bad season, for such seeds lie dormant for several years. Among others, doves eat the horrid, spiky seeds of an abundant ephemeral weed with a yellow flower, aptly called *Tribulus terrestris*. The Namaqua Dove subsists mainly on smaller grass seeds.

Male Namaqua Doves are much prettier and rather larger than the females, with a black forehead and chest, rich metallic purple spots on the wings, and a long black tail. The female is an altogether paler and duller bird, lacking the black breast and forehead, but nevertheless slim and graceful. The long tail is raised and lowered when a Namaqua Dove alights on a bush, presumably as some sort of signal. Most doves give a special call when they alight; but the

The Namaqua Dove

Namaqua Dove has none that is known. Perhaps the long black tail allows it to dispense with any vocal signal.

The voice of the Namaqua Dove is a deep, double coo, "twooh-hoooo", sounding much too portentous for so small a creature. It calls much less often than do other doves of the bush, and is generally heard from within some thicket. Both in voice and appearance it is, in fact, quite distinct from other bush doves; but its nearest relatives are probably the small wood doves, which also have deep mournful voices and cinnamon wings.

Doves and pigeons manage to abound despite what appear to be skimpy and vulnerable nesting habits, and an almost invariable clutch of only two white or buff eggs. The Namaqua Dove is no exception to the general rule, though its nest is slightly better finished than the transparent flimsy structures of some of the turtle doves. Built low in bushes, it is lined with fine rootlets, and the eggs are buff or yellow rather than pure white. The few definite breeding records for East Africa indicate most breeding in the early dry season, in June and July, when seeds of the long rains grass crop are likely to be abundant. In South Africa the breeding season is extended, but more eggs are laid in May, and from September to November than at other times. More records in East Africa will probably reveal that here too this dove can breed in many months, but being a sub-desert bird its breeding season may be more restricted than that of doves of woodland or forest.

Although the male is much more conspicuous than his mate, he shares incubation with her, at least by day; probably she incubates at night. The young hatch in 13–16 days, and are fed by both parents with the usual regurgitated compound known as pigeon's milk, which is secreted by the crop lining, and is unique to this family. They fly in 16 days, and can be distinguished from adults by barring on the underside and having the feathers of the back tipped black, white, and buff – much more spotty and barred in fact.

Doubtless such flimsy nests built low in bushes are accessible to many predators, of which snakes are probably the worst, while small hawks such as the Gabar Goshawk also take many young doves in the nest. However, Namaqua Doves have a short breeding season; and probably if one clutch or brood is lost they can breed again and perhaps succeed this time. Either that, or they must be quite long-lived, which seems unlikely in so small a bird.

The best time to watch doves is at water in the evening sunlight. Arrow straight, they fly in at speed from all around, alight briefly, drink and are gone in a few seconds with a clap of wings. All doves can suck their drink, and do not have to sip, as do most birds; they share this character with sandgrouse. When a Namaqua Dove alights in the sunshine on the edge of a little pool one has a far better opportunity to admire its delicate form and neat but not gaudy plumage than when it is perching in the heat of the day in the interior of a thicket, or flitting briefly away in front of one's car.

Length eight and a half inches, male (nearest) and female

20 The Red-faced Crombec

Sylvietta whytii

There are no nuthatches in Africa south of the Sahara. However, a group of small warblers, known as crombecs or stumptails take their place to some extent, though they do not in fact eat nuts. They are stumpy-tailed, slightly portly little birds that flit about in trees, painstakingly searching crannies in the bark or working along twigs, but also able to take small insect prey from the undersides of the leaves. One or other sort of crombec occurs in most parts of tropical Africa; and the Red-faced Crombec of the bush is both one of the largest and most widespread.

One might describe this delightful little bird as neat, but not gaudy, for its dress is entirely smooth sober grey and rufous-brown, with a brightish rufous face and a sharp slim black bill. Of all the genus, this one resembles a small nuthatch the most, for some of the forest crombecs are much brighter green. It is common and widespread, occurring from West Africa right across to Ethiopia and thence as far south as Moçambique. In South Africa crombecs are firmly called stumptails; and this is a far more descriptive name. This one has practically no visible tail, and rather large broad wings. It occurs in all sorts of country from forest edges to quite arid bush, but is typically a bird of acacia woodland.

Crombecs are often seen by those who camp or idle under a tree and just wait, for they are always on the move, and in due course one, or more likely a pair will arrive in your tree. Once there, they search it most systematically, creeping along boughs in a succession of little hops, flitting to hang briefly from a twig searching small holes in it, finally working up, through and round the leafy canopy. Normally they begin near the bottom of a tree and work right up; and may spend twenty minutes or more in one tree. When they have finished they have found a few insects, spiders and other small things hiding in crevices of bark and clumps of dead leaves that other, more active leaf warblers do not find.

I often have Red-faced Crombecs in my garden. One sometimes comes and works through the flowers outside my study window, at a range of a few feet. I can then see how its bright beady eye is looking up, down, and sideways continually, and how an insect, however

The Red-faced Crombec

secretive, must sometime be found out by that systematic, minutely careful search. They make a speciality of small spiders and moth larvae, but eat other insects too. However, they catch very little active insect prey or much by flying; what they are looking for is things that hide, and escape swifter, flitting birds.

In the rains we become aware of the Crombec in our garden by his loud repeated call, which sounds like "Chi-*preety* chi-*preety* chi-*preety*" repeated five to six times. He calls from high up in trees; and I have generally found this to be true in the bushland also. Thus he advertises his inconspicuous presence in his territory to other crombecs. His mate is much more secretive; and one can have a crombec breeding in the garden for weeks without locating their nest, unless one actually watches them covertly to see where they go.

The nest of all known crombecs are beautifully made and ornamental, but well concealed. The Red-faced Crombec makes a hanging purse nest, usually under the deep shade of a low-growing acacia and attached to a twig near the outer edge of the tree, so that it looks like any bunch of rubbish. One can walk right past a nesting crombec time after time and miss the nest, for the sitting bird slips out very quietly. An attachment is first made with fibres and plenty of cobwebs, and then a small hanging purse built on below. This is made of finer fibres strengthened with plentiful cobwebs. Finally, the outside of the nest is carefully covered with small flakes of lichen, acacia flowers, dead leaves, and tendrils, all bound with web. Most nests are greyish looking, covered with bits of grey lichen and dead leaves; some others, covered with acacia flowers, blobs of resin, and seed pods look yellowish. Apparently an attempt is made to vary the appearance with the locality – or rather, selection operates towards crombecs which make a nest which fits its surroundings. The final construction may look just like an untidy mass of leaves and debris caught in an old spider's web; but is a work of art.

Two eggs are laid as a rule. They are white, spotted and freckled with brown and grey-brown. Everywhere in East Africa they are laid in the rainy months, but in both the long and the short rains. The small clutch of two eggs, and the relatively long breeding season for so small a bird indicates that it actually must be more long-lived on average than most small birds of its size. Either that, or the well-camouflaged nest does give it an advantage in brood survival.

The incubation period is not recorded, but is probably about two weeks. The young remain in the nest for up to seventeen days, so that including the elaborate nest construction it is unlikely that in the short bushland rainy season the Red-faced Crombec could bring off two broods. Care in concealment of the nest is carried right through the fledging period, for in the early stages the parents swallow the droppings of their young, and later on carry them away. A genet cat or mongoose can't locate the nest by a pile of telltale white pellets on the ground.

People are apt to be put off the warblers as an extremely difficult group to identify, partly because of the awful multiplicity in Africa of the grass warblers of the genus *Cisticola*. However, some African warblers are very easily identified, Crombecs amongst them. One might call them the *pons asinorum* of warbler identification; and once they are known, with a few others, that dreadful long list of small brown jobs becomes a little less terrifying.

Length four and a half inches, sexes alike

21 The Freckled Nightjar
Caprimulgus tristigma

Large rocky hills are a feature of the bush all over Africa. Blackish, solid masses of stones and boulders, adorned by a few hardy trees and succulents that cling to their sides where there is soil, they rear fifty, a few hundred, or even a thousand feet out of the plains. The larger are called inselbergs; the smaller, kopjes. They are the ancient eroded stumps of much bigger mountains, and they are the perfect scene for an evening stroll, to watch the sun go down and the bush turn purple, finally shading into soft grey as night falls.

As the dusk draws in you will hear from the rock a clear, emphatic voice. "Whow-how" it says; or "pew-hew, pew-hew-hew". There may be one or there may be many; but if you see the author it will only be a dim flitting form that tells you it is a large nightjar. On moonlight nights the calling continues most of the night; on dark nights it stops almost at once. Such behaviour is typical of nightjars. By night these Freckled Nightjars leave their rock, and hunt insects from open spaces or even roads. At dawn they return, and may call briefly again before disappearing for the day.

Disappear is the word. You know they are on the rock; but you will only find them by chance or, better, by getting up before dawn yourself and watching the bird flit home from the bush below, if you are lucky. When you do see one you will realise why the bird is so hard to find. A marvel of delicate grey vermiculations and blackish spots and bars, the plumage acts as a perfect camouflage. The bird literally melts into its dark rocky background, especially in shade. It knows it, sits absolutely still, and will not finally fly till you are within a few feet. If you were not there its large liquid eye would gleam like a shilling and give it away; but it closes the eye on one side as you approach, and if you could watch as you walk round it you would see one eye slowly closing, the other opening, like the slow waxing or waning of a glowing spark.

Wherever there are rocks in the bush or savanna – not in forest as far as I know – there are Freckled Nightjars. I have found them from Nigeria and Ethiopia to southern Africa. They live only on such rocks; but quite a small one, or a small group of big boulders on the side or

The Freckled Nightjar

top of an otherwise wooded hill will do for a single pair. On a big hump of stone there may be several pairs, and there you will have an evening chorus of "Whow-hows" instead of a single call. Once you know the call the distribution and abundance of the bird becomes clear, though you may never see it. This is the best way to learn about any nightjar's range, for they all have distinctive calls, and utter at dusk.

You may be lucky enough, as I once was on a hill in Nigeria, to find a female sitting on eggs. She sits right out in the open, on a blackish stone slab with no nesting material, practically invisible, and will allow cautious close approach. Should she fly, then the final marvel of camouflage is displayed in the little stone niche where she has chosen to lay her two eggs. Most nightjars eggs are buff, marbled with reddish brown, resembling the earth where they are laid. Hers are grey, marked with darker grey, to match the dark rock. This nightjar has been associated with such rocks through aeons of evolutionary time. Both they and she are ancient features of the bush.

The nest I found in Nigeria was actually the first known. Since then, the Freckled Nightjar has been studied and photographed by Peter Steyn. Since its nesting habitat is completely open, and restricted to rocks, it is an easier nightjar's nest to find than most. The incubating female sits so tight that she can be photographed without a hide; but she does not behave normally in the presence of a human being in the open a few feet away.

The female incubates all day, suffering the full heat of the blazing sun. At dusk the male relieves her, and several changes may occur during the night, a pattern exactly reversing that characteristic of diurnal birds, in which the female normally sits all night. The eggs hatch in about eighteen days, and the young are marvels of camouflage, mottled dark grey and whitish, with down covering most of the shiny bill. They can see and are quite active almost at once. They are fed by the female with regurgitated insects, gripping her bill at the side. The male also feeds, and as the young grow they may be fed every ten minutes or so. Perhaps, as in the European Nightjar, the female lays another clutch before the young of her first are flying, leaving the brood to the male; but there is no proof of this. The young can probably fly at about twenty days old; and by that time are moving actively about their rock slab by night, remaining motionless by day.

It is hard for a human being, with eyesight suited only to strong daylight, to find out what happens at a nightjar's nest. But as I know from experience in Trinidad, it is a special experience to be out alone on a moonlight night, maybe with large animals crashing around, trying desperately to learn, by ear more than by eye, what those mysterious birds are doing. Every birdwatcher should try it at least once.

Length ten inches, male. Courtesy, John G. Tremlett, Esq., Kenya

22 The White-headed Buffalo Weaver
Dinemellia dinemelli

Who Dinemell was I can't think; but he has left his (or her) name for those who like to indulge in a little bit of one-upmanship about one of the commonest, most characteristic birds of the eastern thornbush, from the Sudan and Somalia to northern Tanzania. It is less widespread than the Common or Red-billed Buffalo Weavers (which are probably only one species); and more a bird of arid thornbush of grasslands and cultivation. However, I think most people would agree that of all the birds they see in the thornbush they would remember this one, because it would be one of the first they ever recognised.

If strictly accurate the name is thoroughly misleading in the field. The bird has a white head, true; but what one notices is the bright orange-red rump of both sexes when they rise and fly away. Several other bush birds – such as the White-crowned Shrike and White-crowned Starling – have white heads; but only one this bright red rump, which stands out like a flag. How it evolved is a mystery; but perhaps it is a defensive device which may help to prevent predators from taking an otherwise very conspicuous, large, dark-brown and white bird that feeds in flocks in the open and ought to be a gift for a Gabar Goshawk.

This rather powerful, bold and confiding weaver is highly social in its own habits and consorts with many other species, notably Superb Starlings, White-browed Sparrow Weavers, and White-crowned Starlings. It feeds mainly on the ground, on whatever seeds it can find; but also takes fruit and insects. It quickly becomes tame and visits feeding tables round hotels and lodges, coming to collect crumbs of bread. Although it is so exceedingly common and tame everywhere no one, not even Van Someren (who is often a standby when no one else has recorded anything) seems to have observed this species in any detail. It's the same old story once again.

Males are a good deal bigger and heavier than the somewhat duller females, and have strong, heavy, black bills, while their rumps are a brighter red. There should be absolutely no difficulty in observing these birds because their nests are easy to locate, great masses of sticks

The White-headed Buffalo Weaver

and grass attached to the ends of thorny branches, often quite low down; and the odds are that there will be a mass in or close to the large acacia under which you camp or rest. If you do not immediately see the bird you will soon hear its loud trumpet-like cry, or its confused chattering call. It is likely that even one day's detailed observation at a nest would record a good deal that is essentially new.

This species differs from the commoner black Buffalo Weaver in that in the off season it does not form into large flocks. It is always social; but remains about the same place, and does not wander through the grassland in big groups. This is probably an adaptation to the relative abundance of seed supplies in thornbush as compared to grassland. Yet no one could say that the White-headed Buffalo Weaver is anything but a highly successful bird.

Like most other weavers it breeds in the rains; and the males now show their relationship to the true weavers by hanging from their nests, with waving wings, just as do most Ploceid weavers. The nests themselves are large masses of thorny sticks, often placed on top of a bough and at the very tip. In such situations the bird may pile a rampart of thorny sticks along the bough, which probably helps to prevent attack by small carnivores. If anyone doubts this he can try putting his hand into the entrance of a Buffalo Weaver's nest; it won't come out unscathed, and it is a brave man who will actually feel the eggs. Inside, the nest is well lined with grass and sometimes feathers; and according to Archer in Somalia the nests there are mainly made of grass and not much defended by thorny twigs.

Other Buffalo Weavers are polygamous, males attracting several females to compact nest masses which contain several separate nests. Whether this is true of the White-headed Buffalo Weaver is not known, but it probably is. It is presumably the female who actually lines the nest, as often happens with true weaver birds after the displaying male has attracted a mate. Once the female has lined the nest and laid she is probably responsible thereafter for the whole of the incubation and feeding of the young, as is the case with the common Buffalo Weaver. The young are fed entirely on insects; buffalo weavers seen going to and from grain fields in Ethiopia were feeding not on the ripening grain but on the insects among the leaves and heads.

The nests of White-headed Buffalo Weavers are the favourite roosts and nesting places of Pygmy Falcons. So far as is known, no other breeding site is used by Pygmy Falcons in Somalia or in Kenya. The relationship of the two are obscure; but the White-headed Buffalo Weaver is so large and powerful that it seems unlikely that Pygmy Falcons could take over occupied nest masses, and must use abandoned or empty ones. Perhaps the greater strength and size of the White-headed Buffalo Weaver is one reason why Pygmy Falcons are relatively less common in East Africa than in South Africa, where they can occupy without opposition the nest-chambers of the much smaller Social Weavers.

Length nine inches, sexes alike

23 The White-crowned Shrike
Eurocephalus anguitimens

I suppose, that if I were asked to choose which of the larger bush birds was the most typical and obvious species in the thornbush of East Africa I would probably pick this one. In places, it is extremely common, and moreover is large and conspicuous, perching on the tops of trees. It lives in small parties, and is noisy, calling whenever it takes wing, and is inclined to be social with other species such as buffalo weavers. By now, I should hardly need to add that this common, obvious, relatively large species has apparently never been studied in any detail.

This shrike has a vast range, from the southern Sudan and Ethiopia to the Transvaal and Damaraland. It is normally not found except where there are acacias or other thorny trees, at least mixed with broad-leaved species, and it is most abundant in harsh dry thornbush, in my experience commoner in east and north-east Africa than in south Africa. In the great belt of miombo, or *Brachystegia* woodland that separates the northern and southern thornbush areas, it is found in the swampy valleys between the ridges, because acacias grow in these valleys and *Brachystegia* does not. Thus, it is a species which demonstrates how, in drier epochs, the connection between northern and southern arid belts was clearer and more continuous than it is at present. Naturally, it does perch sometimes on broad leaved trees when these are mixed with acacias; but is generally scarce in broad-leaved long-grass woodland.

By some, this species is divided into two, Ruppell's White-crowned Shrike *L. ruepellii* and the southern White Crowned Shrike *E. anguitimens*. However, it is more usual to lump them together, and I regard this as sound. They are something of an anomaly, being placed nowadays with the helmet shrikes of the genus *Prionops*, but in practice behaving more like an ordinary shrike. Helmet-shrikes also go about in parties; but they move slowly from tree to tree within the cover, and seldom perch much in the open or high up. Several of the true shrikes are also gregarious, and they usually perch in conspicuous high places, so that in some ways the White-crowned Shrike is more like a true shrike than a helmet shrike.

The White-crowned Shrike

Perching as they do on the tops of trees they can easily be mistaken, at first glance, for a Pygmy Falcon, especially from the front. The large heavy head and white front, with the general build, is not unlike it; and I have sometimes wondered whether the shrike is mimicking the Pygmy Falcon or more likely, vice versa. It could be advantageous for the predatory Pygmy Falcon to look like the more harmless shrike. However, once one takes a closer look the white head shows; and as soon as the bird takes flight any resemblance to a Pygmy Falcon is immediately lost. White-crowned Shrikes fly straight, but rather slowly, with rapidly fluttering wings, and often glide to a perch with the wings held high above the back. They accompany this with squeaky cries, the whole performance bearing no resemblance to the swift undulating flight of the Pygmy Falcon, while when they alight the shrikes have no white spots in the tail. Nevertheless, it is interesting that the bird most likely to be confused with this shrike, or vice versa, is the Pygmy Falcon.

These shrikes travel in parties of four to ten or more and feed on insects, which they catch mainly on the ground, but can also catch in the air, for instance flying termites. Most of the food is caterpillars and grasshoppers, but they are said occasionally to take berries. The parties move from tree to tree, feeding as they go. They associate with White-headed Buffalo Weavers and also with White-crowned Starlings in Ethiopia and Somalia, so that care must sometimes be taken to be certain of identification. They are not at all shy, and are very easy to watch, so that it is all the more curious that no one seems to have done so in detail.

Despite its abundance and conspicuous habits, very little is known about the breeding of these birds. There are only about a dozen record cards for the species in the East African nest-record card scheme. These all indicate that it can breed in many months, with a slight peak in both long and short rains. In the harsher climate of Somalia it breeds in and just after the rains, and in southern Africa it breeds chiefly early in the rains, in Rhodesia in October and November. The nest resembles that of a true helmet shrike, a beautiful neat cup, situated in the fork of an acacia branch fifteen or more feet above the ground, made of grass, but covered outside with a felted mass of cobwebs that looks like white clay. The three to five eggs, laid in a shallow cup, are large for the size of the bird, white, mottled and blotched round the larger end with brown and slate-blue. They, and the nest, resemble those of helmet-shrikes rather than true shrikes.

Helmet-shrikes are even more gregarious than White-crowned Shrikes, and also nest in smaller groups together. By reason of their peculiar and rather attractive habits they have been watched more than the much more common and obvious White-crowned Shrikes. I can think of no common, conspicuous bird of the thornbush that would repay more easily a season's concentrated observation than the White-crowned Shrike, for observations on its behaviour would also help to elucidate its true relations with on one hand helmet shrikes, and on the other typical shrikes such as the larger, gregarious Fiscals.

Length nine inches, sexes alike

24　The Golden-breasted Starling
Spreo regius

Driving along a track through the bush one may see a dark, long-tailed, flitting form moving quietly away. It settles on a tree with others of its kind, perhaps in full sun. Out come the binoculars; and if you do not give a satisfied whoop of delight when the full beauty of this glorious bird bursts upon you then I'm not with you. To me, it takes the palm of all the bush birds without difficulty; and it would only be with a wrench that I'd turn it down in favour of the Carmine Bee-eater or Emerald Cuckoo as the most beautiful bird in Africa. Others have their favourites; this is mine, for it combines spectacular beauty of plumage with grace of form, is sufficiently elusive to be something of a prize, and even has a rather sweet voice.

This starling is common and widespread in the bush of north-east Africa but not elsewhere. It and its all sober-grey relative, the Ashy Starling *S. unicolor* which replaces it in southern Tanzania, both used to be in a genus of their own, *Cosmopsarus*, which seems to me more sensible than merging them with the short-tailed genus *Spreo*. Though there are many similarities of habit, there are marked differences also, for these long-tailed starlings are, in general much shyer and more difficult to approach closely and see well than that archetype of *Spreo*, the Superb Starling. Detailed studies of behaviour patterns are needed as well as careful examination of skins in museums, which is the standard method of making such systematic divisions, even now.

A true inhabitant of the dry and desolate thornbush from North Tanzania through Kenya, Somalia, and Ethiopia the Golden-breasted Starling seems almost out of place in these waterless surroundings. However, it is evidently well-adapted and successful, for although it is rather elusive and hard to see well it is certainly common. It moves about through the bush in small parties of up to ten, or in pairs. Occasionally, many collect in a fruiting tree, and those lucky enough to find such an assembly are in for a feast indeed. The starlings may then be quite tame, eager for the fruit; and one can sit under the tree (probably a fig tree) and gaze at close quarters on the glorious contrast of metallic blue back and bright golden chest and

The Golden-breasted Starling

belly, set off by a pale yellow eye, among the green leaves. Seldom does one see them thus, for they usually just flit away in front of you as you struggle through the thorny bush to get a better view.

In aviaries these starlings become very tame, and will perch on a finger to take a meal worm. In the wild they have not been studied in any detail, despite their beauty and the fact that at the nest they are quite confiding and easy to photograph. What little we know suggests that they are mainly insectivorous, taking prey both on the ground and in trees, but well adapted to ground feeding by hopping on their long legs. They tend to roost or rest in company both in the evening, and also in the midday heat, when they keep up a steady low warbling song to one another. Many starlings do this; but these habits remind one more of the Chestnut-winged Starlings of the genus *Onychognathus* than of any species of *Spreo*.

They separate from the flocks into pairs in the breeding season, which occurs in both rains, March to May, and October – December. Nests are made in natural holes of trees, or in old barbet or woodpecker holes, and are lined with grass, roots, and other plant material, sometimes a substantial mass, sometimes only a small pad. In Kenya two to four blue eggs, spotted with brown, are laid; but in Somalia up to six, and broods of six young may be found in the same hole. Nothing in detail seems to be recorded of the incubation habits; but both parents feed the brood, and they are not then difficult to watch, even without a hide. At one observed nest a third adult also fed the young. It is therefore possible that the large broods reared by this species in the short season of abundance may force the habit of communal nesting upon it. However, we need to know much more about it; and anyone who finds a nest can soon add to our knowledge.

Length twelve to fourteen inches, sexes alike

Rèna